SCHOOL CULTURE REWIRED

How to Define, Assess, and Transform It

ASCD MEMBER BOOK

Many ASCD members received this book as a
member benefit upon its initial release.

Learn more at: **www.ascd.org/memberbooks**

SCHOOL CULTURE
REWIRED
How to Define, Assess, and Transform It

STEVE GRUENERT & TODD WHITAKER

Alexandria, Virginia USA

1703 N. Beauregard St. • Alexandria, VA 22311-1714 USA
Phone: 800-933-2723 or 703-578-9600 • Fax: 703-575-5400
Website: www.ascd.org • E-mail: member@ascd.org
Author guidelines: www.ascd.org/write

Judy Seltz, *Executive Director;* Stefani Roth, *Publisher;* Genny Ostertag, *Director, Content Acquisitions;* Julie Houtz, *Director, Book Editing & Production;* Ernesto Yermoli, *Editor;* Donald Ely, *Senior Graphic Designer;* Mike Kalyan, *Manager, Production Services;* Cynthia Stock, *Production Designer;* Kelly Marshall, *Production Specialist*

All referenced trademarks are the property of their respective owners.

All web links in this book are correct as of the publication date below but may have become inactive or otherwise modified since that time. If you notice a deactivated or changed link, please e-mail books@ascd.org with the words "Link Update" in the subject line. In your message, please specify the web link, the book title, and the page number on which the link appears.

PAPERBACK ISBN: 1-978-1-4166-1990-1   ASCD product #115004
Quantity discounts: 10–49, 10%; 50+, 15%; 1,000+, special discounts
(e-mail programteam@ascd.org or call 800-933-2723, ext. 5773, or 703-575-5773).
Also available in e-book formats. For desk copies, go to www.ascd.org/deskcopy.

ASCD Member Book No. FY15-4A (Jan. 2015 PSI+). Member books mail to Premium (P), Select (S), and Institutional Plus (I+) members on this schedule: Jan, PSI+; Feb, P; Apr, PSI+; May, P; Jul, PSI+; Aug, P; Sep, PSI+; Nov, PSI+; Dec, P. For details, see www.ascd.org/membership and www.ascd.org/memberbooks.

Library of Congress Cataloging-in-Publication Data
Gruenert, Steve.
    School culture rewired : how to define, assess, and transform it / by Steve Gruenert and Todd Whitaker.
        pages cm
    Includes bibliographical references and index.
    ISBN 978-1-4166-1990-1 (alk. paper)
    1. Educational leadership. 2. School management and organization. 3. School environment. 4. Educational change. I. Whitaker, Todd, 1959– II. Title.
    LB2805.G78 2014
    370.15'8—dc23
                                                                                2014037450

23 22 21 20 19 18 17 16 15   2 3 4 5 6 7 8 9 10 11 12

SCHOOL CULTURE REWIRED
How to Define, Assess, and Transform It

CHAPTER 1

Defining Organizational Culture

*H*ave you ever noticed how service can vary from restaurant to restaurant? At some, you walk in and are greeted by a friendly, attractive host who whisks you away to an available table; at others, you can't get anyone to make eye contact with you, let alone greet you in a friendly way. Often, such a disparity can be found among restaurants that are part of the same chain! What is going on? How can two restaurants from the same company be so dramatically different?

Similar disparities can be found between and within schools and districts: You walk into some schools and immediately feel welcome; you walk into others and you feel like an intruder. In some schools, every teacher seems to be out from behind the desk, lessons are infused with technology, and students appear to be highly engaged in learning; in others, teachers seem to use their desks as fortresses and students appear distracted or disengaged. In both schools, teachers will tell you that what they're doing is effective.

Why is it that some schools embrace new ideas, while others consider them distractions? Why do some teachers roll up their sleeves, while others simply roll their eyes? More important, is there anything we can do to address these differences? Often, disparities within schools and districts are the result of separate cultures having been established over time. For schools to be effective, educators need to understand the organizational cultures in which they work and be able to modify them if necessary.

Understanding an Elusive Concept

This book is intended to help you better understand the general concept of school culture, learn the strengths and weaknesses of your specific school culture, and—perhaps most important—influence your school culture or, if necessary, shape a new one (see Figure 1.1). In the following pages, you'll learn what to do, what to expect, and what positive and negative signs to look out for when trying to improve your school's culture.

Fig 1.1 The Keys to Shaping a New School Culture

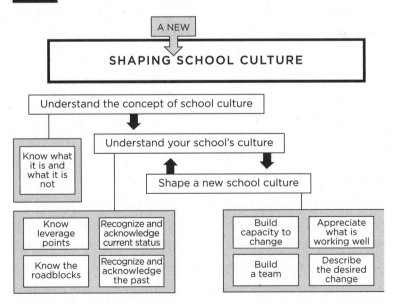

To improve your school culture, you must dig deep into the psyche of your organization and figure out why certain actions or attitudes are entrenched. Often, such actions or attitudes are actually rewarded by a school's culture, so any desirable new behaviors will need to be rewarded by the culture as well if they are to be sustained. Indeed, the effect of school culture on teacher and student behaviors cannot be understated.

You may be thinking, *But surely people choose what to do in every situation—it's not as though we're robots programmed to act a certain way when we arrive at school, right?* The fact is, the whole purpose of a school culture is to get members to adopt predictable behaviors and a common mental model. Culture is both a survival mechanism and a framework for solving problems. If every member of a group agrees to fulfill a certain role within the group, then the group has a better chance of surviving. If some members stray from their roles, the group becomes weak; if many stray or even defect from the group, the group becomes vulnerable to takeover. In the context of schools, a takeover could mean the ascension of a new leader who is not very effective. So, yes—in a sense, culture *is,* as Hofstede put it, a "collective programming of the mind which distinguishes the members of one organization from another" (1997, p. 180). Cultural programming even provides members with virus protection in the form of immunity from external influence. To a culture, any change is a virus.

The effectiveness of a new culture depends on the strength of the people behind the change and the strength of the pre-existing culture. For example, imagine that a new, charismatic leader arrives at a school with a weak pre-existing culture lacking cohesiveness. Using a few persuasive tricks to hook teachers emotionally, such a leader might convince the faculty to gel around his or her values, which eventually will freeze into a school culture (Lewin, 1951). If the leader is sufficiently charismatic, the new culture might become strong and difficult to change—bad news if his or her values are misguided or counterproductive. However, if you and your colleagues have a real understanding of what a school culture is, you'll be a lot less likely to let a misguided leader take over your school.

The effectiveness of a new culture depends on the strength of the people behind the change and the strength of the pre-existing culture.

Look around you—the call for accountability has brought an urgency to schools that feels more like panic. Educators have been convinced that they're doing a poor job and have been sold the idea that they'll benefit from leadership informed by business practices. As the line of ineffective corporate leaders gets longer, MBAs who can't achieve success in the corporate world are increasingly entering the field of education, but this is hardly ever a good fit. The culture of schools, like the culture of churches or community centers, is a world away from the culture of Big Business. Whereas churches and community centers are usually nonprofit organizations that provide desired services to the local population, corporations seek beyond all else to make a profit. Which of these two missions better represents what schools should hope to do?

How the Experts Define Culture

Edgar Schein, Geert Hofstede, Clifford Geertz, Terry Deal, and Allen Kennedy are just a few of the major names in the study of organizational culture, which has its roots in the field of sociology. Geertz has noted that culture "is not a part of experimental science in search of laws but an interpretive one in search of meaning" (Geertz, 1973, p. 5). Culture is not a problem that needs to be solved, but rather a framework that a group can use to solve problems; it is how we learn to survive, one generation passing down what it has learned to the next. Culture is essentially a social indoctrination of unwritten rules that people learn as they try to fit in a particular group (Schein, 1992). It's also been referred to at different times as any of the following:

- The social glue that holds people together
- "The way we do things around here"
- Activity behind the scenes or between the lines
- What's *really* going on
- The patterns of behavior that distinguish *us* from *them*
- An invisible force-field that limits actions and thoughts
- A set of behaviors that seem strange to new employees
- Deeply embedded beliefs and assumptions
- The unwritten rules
- Software for the mind
- A home-court feeling
- The default mode of behavior

- Covert assimilation (that feels like accommodation)
- A collective consciousness
- Shared social reflexes
- The "box" that we try to think outside of
- Proof that organizations can learn
- A code honored by members
- A latent system of authority

Culture is a social narcotic to which practically all of us are addicted—we feel good when we belong to a group. Members of a culture will help to shape one another, and the culture in turn will evolve into a unique group of individuals who share certain characteristics and take some pride in being set apart from those outside the group. (You can very clearly see this dynamic in action among student cliques and subcultures.) An organizational culture develops as the group responds to any challenges in its environment; as Hofstede (1997) put it, "When people are moved as individuals, they will adapt to the culture of their new environment; when they are moved as groups, they will bring their own culture along" (p. 201).

The fundamental question that school leaders should ask themselves regarding their school cultures is this: Is it something we can predict and control, or does it control us? Put another way: Is it the sentry at the door or the monster under the bed? In the pages that follow, we'll present strategies for making sure that your school culture is positive, healthy, and adaptable to new challenges.

CHAPTER 2

Culture vs. Climate

One of the best ways to understand the concept of school *culture* is to contrast it with the concept of school *climate*. Though both are important, a school's climate is both a window into its culture and a learned response that the culture teaches new members. Figure 2.1 shows some ways of distinguishing between the two concepts.

Fig 2.1 **Some Differences Between Climate and Culture**

Culture . . .	Climate . . .
. . . is the group's personality.	. . . is the group's attitude.
. . . gives Mondays permission to be miserable.	. . . differs from Monday to Friday, February to May.
. . . provides for a limited way of thinking.	. . . creates a state of mind.
. . . takes years to evolve.	. . . is easy to change.
. . . is based on values and beliefs.	. . . is based on perceptions.
. . . can't be felt, even by group members.	. . . can be felt when you enter a room.
. . . is part of us.	. . . surrounds us.
. . . is "the way we do things around here."	. . . is "the way we feel around here."
. . . determines whether or not improvement is possible.	. . . is the first thing that improves when positive change is made.
. . . is in your head	

Personality vs. Attitude

If culture is a school's personality, climate is its attitude. The biggest difference between the two is that an attitude is far easier to change than a personality. Need proof? Simply announce to the school that tomorrow is a snow day and you might notice a sudden change in climate as educators' and students' attitudes suddenly lift. The promise of a snow day doesn't change the school's personality (i.e., culture), but the collective shift in attitude (i.e., climate) *allows the school to reveal what it values.* In this case, the school climate reveals that the culture values not being in school. Of course, changing a personality requires a more purposeful and sustained effort than does changing an attitude.

If you want to bust a culture . . .
Ask teachers why they like snow days.

Morale as a Barometer of Culture

Morale—the degree of happiness among school staff—is particularly reflective of a school's culture and has a very strong effect on school climate. Setting the morale in a building is a 24/7 process; it can't be done by a one-off faculty dinner, raffle, or retreat. And morale can change quickly: When numbers become more important than people, when spreadsheets replace stories, when the group feels divided by unfair treatment, when the future simply seems bleak—it's at these times that leaders can prove their effectiveness. Positive school leaders who care about their staff can rally the troops, comfort those who are experiencing uncertainty, and generally try to change the climate by lifting morale. Negative school leaders can also rally the troops, but in their case it's to agree that they're all victims of a dysfunctional system. Whether for good or for ill, the school climate will reflect a change in morale, which can itself only occur if the culture allows it.

How Culture Gives Us Permission to Be Miserable

Monday is not an *inherently* bad day; it just so happens that, for most of us, it marks the beginning of the typical work week after two days of rest. As a result, many teachers are more lethargic and reluctant to work on Mondays than during the rest of the week. Some teachers are practically useless on Mondays—not because they are actually tired, but because that is how they feel they are *supposed* to act.

Now, imagine that a teacher enters school on a cold and rainy February morning in a good mood—she loves her work, her students, and her colleagues, and she shows it. As she walks toward her classroom with a smile on her face and some pep in her step, how do you imagine that her colleagues might react? They might wonder what's wrong with her. Some might even ask, "What are you so happy about?" They might be smiling as they do it, but deep down they hope that she'll become as disgruntled as they are. And just the opposite happens on Friday afternoons: Those who love their jobs and therefore don't want to rush out of the building as soon as the buses leave are ostracized for not conforming to a culture that expects them to do so. This is because singling out positive teachers makes negative teachers feel better *by reinforcing a negative culture.*

A school culture might encourage a miserable mindset on Mondays and a can't-wait-to-leave mindset on Fridays among teachers *even when the mindsets don't conform to the teachers' true feelings.* More crucially, a culture that encourages such an outlook is essentially telling students that they, too, should not want to be in school and should spend their schooldays impatient for the weekend. Culture conveys to its members what they ought to celebrate, ignore, or anticipate.

If you want to bust a culture . . . *Celebrate Mondays.*

Consider the following example of climate informing culture. Many teachers consider student assemblies to be a waste of time. When a critical mass of teachers at a school adopts such an attitude, a climate of apathy is bound to reign during assemblies. The overarching culture may then use this apathy to possibly discredit the people who set up the assemblies, or perhaps to suggest that other school functions are wastes of time, too. If this happens, it's proof that the school culture is dysfunctional.

Values are often unconscious to those who hold them and thus difficult to articulate to others. However, values *can* be observed by outsiders and inferred by the way we act under different circumstances, the structures in place at our school, and the way we use our resources. The difficulty of articulating values is precisely what helps to make them sustainable (Argyris, 2010). This is a problem if you want to shape a new culture. Negative teachers who enjoy the fruits of dysfunction as an excuse to do nothing will not want their true values revealed.

If you want to bust a culture . . . *Praise and compliment risk taking.*

A State of Mind That Is Stuck in a Box

When people try to "think outside the box," the culture of which they are a part *is that box.* Like religion or other traditions passed down along generations, culture provides us with a mental security blanket of sorts. Wandering outside of the box may be perceived as an act of creativity, but only for a little while—one cannot live outside the box and still maintain all the rights and privileges associated with staying inside of it. The pressure to remain within the box is what Elder and Paul (2012) call *sociocentric thinking*: "The tendency to internalize group norms and beliefs, take on group identities, and act as we are expected to act—without the least sense that what we are doing might reasonably be questioned" (p. 22). Culture, therefore, defines what it means to be normal.

We tend to gravitate toward groups—that is, cultures—that share our beliefs, preferences, or goals. Doing so enhances our sense of security and self-esteem. Within cultures, subcultures may exist of members who share more values or interests with one another than they do with the rest of the group. As members of a culture, we learn to react in specific ways when particular events occur: with sympathy when someone gets hurt, happiness when our team wins, anger when we have to wait for things, and so on. By reacting in the expected manner, we telegraph our commitment to the culture's values. For example, in some schools, teachers might be expected to exhibit relief when a challenging student is expelled, and so they may do so even if they don't feel any relief at all. (In fact, they may feel as though they themselves failed the student.) Or consider faculty meetings: At many schools, the culture is to summarily dread such meetings, even if they may actually be fun and collegial affairs. Over time, teachers who work in such cultures will convince themselves that the meetings are really just a waste of time.

If you want to bust a culture . . .
Have fun in meetings that aren't supposed to be fun.

Shifting from Climate to Culture

Whereas a change in climate can occur instantly, a change in culture is necessarily a slow evolution. If, starting tomorrow, a heretofore distant principal decides to act in a positive and friendly manner, others may quickly adopt similar behavior and the school climate will have suddenly changed. If the principal soon reverts back to her previous attitude, the force of the school culture will strongly encourage everyone else to revert back as well; if, however, she sticks to the new attitude for the long run, then positivity and friendliness will slowly become entrenched as a part of the school culture. It can be hard to tell precisely when a shift from climate to culture—that is, from short-term behaviors to long-term expectations—occurs.

School leaders who decide to implement cultural change should understand that the culture will take many years to reflect new beliefs that guide behaviors to the point where they are like second nature. Leaders can build structures and change procedures to shape the new culture, but they often try to do too much too soon; the real test will come when nobody is looking.

If you want to bust a culture . . . *Ask educators why cultural change takes so long.*

Perceptions vs. Values and Beliefs

One of the things that makes culture so difficult to change is that it's so hard for us to pinpoint—it is always easier to describe *what you do* (climate) rather than *why you do it* (culture). Visitors to a school are often the ones who can sense the school's culture the most. For example, substitute teachers may feel the uniqueness of each school's culture better than staff do, because they have such a breadth of reference points to which they can compare it. Similarly, new employees will initially notice the differences between their new school and previous ones; however, as they begin to fit in—as the culture teaches them and reinforces how to act at faculty meetings, when to show up at work, how to dress, when to send a kid to the office, and so on—the uniqueness of the new culture will gradually dissipate as the culture eventually become "the new normal."

If you want to bust a culture . . . *Try new teaching methods.*

Climate Is Around Us—Culture Is Part of Us

Culture provides a school's identity and image—its "brand." Though teachers may criticize what their school does, they probably wouldn't tolerate outsiders criticizing their school.

Cultural artifacts are all around us—in the trophy case, in the alignment of desks in classrooms, in the amount of time provided for lunch, in the types of student data we collect, in what we laugh at. Culture tells us when to be tense and when to relax and rewards us for acting appropriately, usually in the form of greater security, more self-esteem, or access to inside information.

As with culture, climate is not a problem that needs to be solved; rather, it simply indicates the type of culture we may have, and it allows us to diagnose the effects of any strategies we might use to change the culture.

If you want to bust a culture . . .
Visit other, more effective schools.

Culture Has Enemies—Climate Does Not

For solidarity to develop in a culture, there needs to be a common enemy. The bonding necessary for a group to become a team requires goals, the foremost of which is simply to survive. The enemies of any given culture will be the people or forces that try to change it. Changing a culture into something different is the same as destroying the old one. These forces of change can emerge from other cultures, from subcultures within the parent culture, or from individuals.

Climate is the culmination of the collective attitudes of the members of a group. It is how most of us feel most of the time in certain situations. There will always be moments when it seems as though the climate is changing; at these times, it may feel like the entire culture has shifted. However, these changes usually occur *within the boundaries of the culture*. A culture allows the climate to be sensitive during certain situations; it allows people to get emotional and react impulsively, but not unpredictably. There is always a range of accepted behaviors for any situation that the culture will allow.

Climate does not have enemies. That would not make sense. It is the reflection of a group response, much like applause at a music performance or gasps when our team loses a game.

It would be pointless to resent the response; what we may resent are the conditions leading to it. Culture tells us when to applaud—this is why people will look around to make sure that applause is acceptable at a given point during a performance. If we are the performers and applause is either lukewarm or absent, we are not angry with the dearth of the applause itself, but rather with *what that absence represents*—a value system (culture) at odds with our performance.

If you want to bust a culture . . . *Push the boundaries of culturally acceptable behaviors.*

Culture Defines What It Means to Be Normal

Deal and Kennedy (1982) described culture most aptly when they referred to culture as "the way we do things around here" (p. 4). A culture defines normalcy and morality for its members. Although many schools have very similar sets of policy in place, how those policies are implemented and enforced is ultimately what sets school cultures apart. Remember: When it comes to school culture, unwritten rules always trump the written rules. Regardless of what policies may be written in a school's handbook, it's the cultural interpretation of those policies that most helps teachers know how they are expected to act.

"How we do things around here" is usually the first lesson new teachers at a school receive. To gain membership in the new culture, they will need to know this information. To be validated as a real teacher in the eyes of the school, they will need to display the behaviors and beliefs expected from them.

Of course, every school culture includes subcultures composed of teachers with different strengths. For example, there may be a subculture in your school composed of teachers who are particularly effective at disciplining students. Administrators would do well to encourage new teachers to seek out and join such a subculture. If there is no such subculture at your school, it may be time to develop one; as we will discuss later in this book, encouraging a subculture of especially competent teachers can be key to creating a new and improved overall school culture.

If you want to bust a culture . . . *Encourage the development of a subculture of your most effective teachers.*

Culture, Climate, and School Improvement

The term "school improvement" has gotten a bad rap lately, conjuring as it does themes like accountability, compliance, and remediation—sounds about as fun as a trip to the dentist. But improvement should be viewed positively; after all, the very point of education is to use available resources to improve the quality of life for all. Unfortunately, toxic school cultures encourage individuals to see failures as the inevitable results of circumstances outside of their control rather than as opportunities for improvement. It's easy to blame students' poverty or special needs for failure, thus letting teachers off the hook for poor performance and setting lower expectations for achievement. Individuals who wish to improve their performance, especially those who are very good at their craft, need to reflect on weak performances and ask themselves, "What did I do wrong?" Failure provides us with the opportunity to step back and realize that something needs to change. Educators in healthy school cultures understand the power of failure and will actively search for these opportunities even if it means confronting their own disappointments. It is the culture that determines whether failures will constitute steps forward or backward for staff.

A school culture may try to sell the concept of school improvement as a series of subtle adaptations to current practice that don't contradict the school's existing value system rather than adopting a new value system altogether. It's always easier to improve existing conditions than to institute fundamental change—although most school cultures prefer simply to maintain the status quo. One strategy for keeping things as they are is to make certain topics, such as cultural change, verboten (Argyris, 2010). People will learn to avoid the elephant in the room. A negative culture reinforces the idea that any dysfunction the school faces is totally normal. The slightest suggestion that things should change at all will be seen as a sacrilegious attack on the school's value system.

If you want to bust a culture . . . *Ask who will keep us from improving.*

Climate and Culture Both Reside in Our Minds

Climate and culture are both constructs that we use to describe how we interact with our environment. Culture influences our values and beliefs; climate constitutes those values and beliefs in action. However, there are times when, by adjusting the climate, we can actually begin to change portions of the culture.

Consider, for example, a school with a lax dress code. The dress code is a function of the school's culture; when there are no scheduled outside visitors at the school, the school climate—lots of jeans and T-shirts—will naturally reflect the culture. Now, imagine that teachers at the school dress more formally when visitors are around, passing it off as their regular mode of dress. In this case, the usual climate changes *because this is what the culture tells us to do when we have visitors.* Thus, the more visitors the school has, the more often staff will dress more formally—creating a pattern that extends over a significant period of time that can potentially change part of the culture. Positive reinforcement by school leaders—complimenting staff when they're gussied up, for example—can lead to teachers eventually dressing up even when no visitors are on site.

As Hofstede, Hofstede, and Minkov (2010) put it, culture is the software for the mind—it is the operating program that the group provides you with to support it. By contrast, climate is what shows up on your computer desktop. Culture massages the data from the environment you take in and then limits your choice of responses to each situation. Climate is the sum of responses.

Reality is a matter of interpretation—it's a collection of memories in our minds. Culture provides us with categories for those memories; it helps us to determine what we see. When we are aware of why we do the things we do, we can no longer do them unthinkingly (Ray, 2001). Once we learn about our culture, we can no longer be its victims because we have choices—comply with it, change it, or leave.

If you want to bust a culture . . .
Ask people to explain the elephant in the room.

CHAPTER 3

Building Blocks
and Subcultures

Whenever people spend a significant amount of time together in a group, they tend to learn what different group members' strengths are and assign roles based on them, thus ensuring some predictability as they try to survive their environment together. To preserve both the group and their own membership within the group, members will do what they can to fit into their roles. This can occur without a leader standing up and telling everyone it needs to happen; it is a natural process that we are hard-wired to accept (Bohannan, 1995). A leader can help to create a culture by bringing a cause to the attention of a group of people, developing a following, identifying an enemy, imposing rules, and recruiting more members. This is true of all organizations, whether they're high-functioning or not. Even cults get started this way.

Each of us has developed patterns of behavior with which we are comfortable. If a school culture is strong, members of the school will have an idea of what other members are going to say in a given situation. This kind of predictability provides a sense of comfort within the group: Even if we know Mr. Jones will have a negative response to the idea of peer observations, being able to predict as much helps us to feel socially secure.

Imagine for a moment that a substantive change occurs at your school—a change in grading policies, perhaps, or in the teacher dress code. Would you be able to predict how each teacher might react to this change? Your ability to do so and to use this knowledge to improve your school is critical.

No school starts with a clean slate. Even brand-new schools have a culture in place, made up of the values and beliefs that staff members bring with them. Veteran teachers will bring some of their previous school culture; new teachers will bring the values that they were taught in school. Because such a culture is fragmented, it's easier to shape into something new.

Just about everything that goes on in a school is a function of the school's culture to some degree. As leaders, we know this to be true; as scientists, we struggle to empirically prove that culture even exists. Writers such as Seymour Sarason, Michael Fullan, Andy Hargreaves, Mike Schmoker, Terry Deal, and Kent Peterson all agree that culture is both very important for lead-

---

Just about everything that goes on in a school is a function of the school's culture to some degree.

---

ers to understand and also a difficult topic to pin down. School leaders have known for a long time that *something* is influencing teachers' working methods—the degree to which they make an effort, the fidelity with which they implement new ideas, the attitudes that they have toward parents, these are all held in check by some kind of force. Leaders have three choices when they discover such a force: they can ignore it, fight it, or use it.

The Building Blocks of School Culture

Cultures are made up of building blocks in the form of all the elements that make life comfortable, predictable, and safe for us. At work, we come to depend on the people around us as they fulfill their culturally assigned roles. These performances provide a rhythm or flow to the day that contributes to our own efficiency and sanity. To understand these elements is to know who is a member of the culture and who is not.

Leaders need to have a big-picture view of their school, which they can only attain if they're able to sufficiently remove themselves from the school culture's grip and examine what holds it together. For such a perspective to make sense, we need to break culture down to its discrete elements (Geertz, 1973). The following elements are especially instructive when analyzing a school's culture:

- Climate
- Mission and vision
- Language
- Humor
- Routines, rituals, and ceremonies
- Norms
- Roles
- Symbols
- Stories
- Heroes
- Values and beliefs

Climate

Because many aspects of a school's culture start out as behavioral or attitudinal issues, addressing school climate is a good strategy for assessing and leveraging cultural change. We can change behaviors and attitudes by employing specific leadership strategies. Over time, if these changes are sustained, the new behaviors or attitudes will become a part of the culture, thus relieving leaders of having to manage them and making them essential. *The culture wants to manage the organization.*

Addressing school climate is a good strategy for assessing and leveraging cultural change.

Here's an example of what we mean. If a principal asks teachers not to use sarcasm with students, most of the teachers will comply. If compliance persists, the school culture itself will begin to devalue the use of sarcasm with students, making the principal's work easier. This is how culture can be made to work for leaders—once something becomes embedded in the culture, it becomes very difficult to remove it or even alter it.

Here's another example. Imagine that a veteran teacher with a strong personality is dismissive toward a parent's concerns. The principal shows indifference to the situation, and a few other teachers support their colleague. Over time, a climate that makes parents feel uncomfortable when they challenge a teacher will become the norm—the school culture, in which new teachers are expected to devalue parental concerns, will discourage parental input. (Some teachers may secretly hope that certain parents don't attend Open House night or parent-teacher conferences while publicly deriding these same parents for not being involved in their kids' education. "What am I supposed to do with Billy?" they might say. "His parents never even come to Open House night!")

Mission and Vision

Culture represents the unwritten mission of the school—it tells students and staff why they are there. Mission statements don't matter much; what does matter is the degree to which leadership and faculty are emotionally invested in the mission (Turner, 2013). By clarifying our roles in the school, a mission can help to make our work easier. Because the purpose of a mission is to institutionalize a set of beliefs and behaviors, it must be aligned with the school culture. If there's a conflict between mission and culture, the latter always wins out.

Culture represents the unwritten mission of the school—it tells students and staff why they are there.

If a mission clarifies our purpose in the school—why we are here—a school's vision is an idea of what it hopes to eventually become. Cultures have missions, but they do not have visions—they can only perceive themselves as they currently are, not as they will be. The culture exists to manage the organization in its present state. If we could talk to the culture, the future would be clear: The culture would tell us, *just repeat the past*. Only leaders can have visions that might potentially change the culture. Cultures do not lead; leaders lead. If the culture is leading, then the leader is only managing.

Organizational visions need to inspire action. To do this, they need to counter the current culture to some degree. A strong vision works better when it can build upon past successes rather than elaborate on past failures and offer a peek into a future that doesn't scare school staff. To visualize a better

---

A strong vision works better when it can build upon past successes rather than elaborate on past failures.

---

school culture is not to discredit the current one too much, as that would create animosity among those who've worked so hard to maintain the status quo.

Language

The language we use within a school can help to delineate the boundaries between those who are a part of the culture and those who aren't. Just as learning a foreign language helps us absorb the culture the language is rooted in, the particular jargon or turns of phrase associated with a school can help us to absorb that school's culture. And just as there are various dialects within foreign countries, there are often distinct "local" vocabularies in schools that separate, say, 4th grad-ers from kindergarteners or math teachers from the fine-arts faculty. Teachers of special education are especially prone to being separated from their colleagues by language as they tend to live by specialized descriptions, interventions, and strate-gies, many of them shrouded in acronyms. Because they are often separated from other teachers in the school and deal with especially challenging students, special education teach-ers often will enjoy a camaraderie among themselves that can unintentionally set them apart from everyone else. The acronyms and jargon of our workplace help to tell us who is informed and who is not and offer faculty a sense of comfort and competence as they go about solving problems. To not understand the local language is to demonstrate a lower level of usefulness in the eyes of the culture.

To not understand the local language is to demonstrate a lower level of usefulness in the eyes of the culture.

Humor

What people find amusing can also separate cultural insiders from outsiders. Although some jokes are funny no matter who you are, others have punch lines that only a select group will understand. When we laugh along with others, it is a sign that we are all on the same page—we have something in common and can proceed with the social contract. Our body language when responding to humor can often be enough to reaffirm a bond with others even if we don't say a word.

Small talk is supposed to be light—rarely is it acceptable to launch into deep, philosophical issues when simply socializing. Getting others to laugh at something we have said makes us feel as though we've been accepted—even, at times, when the joke's on us. Here's an example. A principal was once approached by an extremely angry parent. In the hallway, she called him every unpleasant thing that came to her mind. The entire time that she was yelling at him, all he could think of was the piece of raw chicken sitting on her shoulder, left there from the night shift she worked at the local slaughterhouse. When her tirade was over, she walked out the door without listening to any response. As he stood there in disbelief, a veteran teacher came up to him, patted him on the back, and said with a smile, "Welcome to the club." Certainly that was not the first time she had created that experience for an administrator, and as we think about it, it was one of many experiences he probably had to endure to gain the trust of the faculty. The experience became a source of humor at many future faculty meetings, yet he welcomed the laughter that it caused because it meant that he was now a member of the club.

Routines, Rituals, and Ceremonies

Routines can become rituals, which can in turn transform into ceremonies. Routines are those things we do every day to ensure that the school is efficiently run; by contrast, rituals are stylized public expressions of our values and beliefs. A routine can be made into ritual if it represents a strong value in the school—taking attendance, for example. What begins as a quick, non-disruptive, reflexive action can become a public expression if we decide that it needs attention.

Routines ensure that days follow a pattern so that we can occasionally turn on auto-pilot as we go about our work. When our daily rhythm aligns with the organizational flow of events, it's as though we're all dancing to the music—the culture—

Routines are those things we do every day to ensure that the school is efficiently run; by contrast, rituals are stylized public expressions of our values and beliefs.

---

that we perceive. Routines can be informal: some teachers may routinely meet for coffee or lunch. And just as golfers have pre-shot routines, teachers may have pre-teaching routines that get them into the right frame of mind to teach effectively. (Some teachers may not even realize that they do this!)

Rituals are collective dramas of persuasion—they make statements about the quality of life and set standards for behavior (Kuh & Whitt, 1988). Rituals are actions common to enough members of a culture that they calcify norms. Some rituals may be technically unnecessary for reaching our professional goals, but we engage in them because we consider them to be socially essential—good for sustaining the culture.

Ceremonies are simply glorified rituals—they are regularly held events that usually incorporate visitors to the school in recognizing an important aspect of the school culture. Ceremonies usually include formal protocols and a sense of pageantry. Examples of common school ceremonies include graduations, retirement dinners, class reunions, installations of new board members, and celebrations for reaching school goals. (At some schools, just about every athletic event is a ceremony.)

Rituals can become ceremonies when the leadership chooses to glorify certain values by spotlighting certain behaviors. A faculty meeting can become a ceremony if the principal decides to recognize a teacher's exemplary performance; a teacher can make a ceremony out of sending a student to the office. Routines become rituals, rituals become ceremonies—it's up to the principal to decide how these things evolve. (If rituals and ceremonies stir up images of religious events, it's not a coincidence—many of them exist to acknowledge values that the school considers "sacred.")

Norms

Norms are the unwritten rules that maintain coherence within a group, and they often trump the written rules. Learning norms help members fit in—they help them know when they need to show up, how fast they should work, and when it's time to go home. Norms provide the standards of conduct that help members understand what the group values—they tell us when it is time to be serious, joke around, or be emotional.

In schools, norms can make or break new initiatives, new employees, or new leaders. If written policies are like speed limits, unwritten norms are the average actual speed at which the cars are going: If the speed limit is 55 miles per hour but most people are driving 70 miles per hour, then it's safer go 70 than 55. The culture will determine the true pace; to deviate from it can be harmful.

In schools, norms can make or break new initiatives, new employees, or new leaders.

The culture of any organization is shaped by the worst behavior the leader is willing to tolerate. The rules may state that employees must be at work by 7:30, but whatever time the tardiest employee is allowed to show up without being sanctioned may become the norm if no action is taken.

Roles

Norms help us know our roles in the organization. Some teachers may fill the role of comedian during faculty meetings; others may fill the role of defender of athletics whenever the department is challenged; still others may take on the role of remaining quiet and not voicing an opinion. Cultures find ways of reminding members what their roles are whenever they try to step out of them. If the quiet teacher attempts to share an opinion, others may act surprised—a subtle reminder to the quiet person that he or she is deviating from his or her established role in the culture.

Symbols

Symbols are words, gestures, pictures, or objects that carry a particular meaning that is only recognized by those who share the culture (Geertz, 1973). Symbols answer the question, "What do we value the most around here?" They do not so much reflect reality as translate it into a form that can be shared and understood by others (Kuh & Whitt, 1988).

Symbols can be trademarks used to represent a brand, such as the Nike swoosh or the BMW logo. In schools, symbols can take the shape of mascots, school songs, memorials, trophies, and so on—those things that represent what the school culture values most. Like rituals, symbols are more "visible to an outside observer; their cultural meaning, however, is invisible and lies precisely and only in the ways these practices are interpreted by insiders" (Hofstede, 1997, p. 8). For example, if we were to ask teachers in a school why there is a trophy case by the front door, they'd probably tell us that it's because they think it's important to proudly display the students' accomplishments.

Stories

Stories serve at least five organizational functions:

1. Providing information about a culture's rules,
2. Keeping institutional memory sharp,
3. Increasing commitment and loyalty,
4. Reinforcing artifacts of the culture, and
5. Connecting current faculty with the institution's past. (Kuh & Whitt, 1988)

Stories constitute the qualitative side of life; they provide the context by which we let others know what and who is important. As Kuh and Witt (1988) put it, "Myths, as a form of story, help to rationalize a turbulent external environment and enrich the life of the institution" (p. 22).

Stories are the currency of a culture—they are the most effective means of transferring information from one person to another. Like culture, stories live in people's minds. Leaders use stories to illuminate and illustrate what members of a group need to do to become successful. We tell stories to others and to ourselves as a way of supporting our belief systems.

Fear is a great motivator: If the veteran teacher's story to the new teacher saves him or her from harm, then the culture wins.

Neither stories nor myths need to be true to serve their function. By the time a story has been told over the course of a few generations, there may be little truth left to it. Some leaders use stories to give life to a vision; others use them to share what has happened in the past. Stories about past events that shaped where we are today can limit where we hope to go in the future. They also let us know who or what the enemies of the group are. Stories are essentially the culture's handbook, featuring policies and procedures embedded in fables of courage and resilience. The stories we choose to tell and the embellishments we make to them will depend on the effect we want to have. A veteran staff member might relate a story to a new teacher about the time someone tried a particular teaching strategy and infuriated the principal as a way of dissuading him or her from trying it. Fear is a great motivator: If the veteran teacher's story to the new teacher saves him or her from harm, then the culture wins.

Heroes

Heroes are those people—dead or alive, real or imaginary—who possess characteristics that are highly prized in a culture and thus serve as models for behavior (Deal & Kennedy, 1982). Heroes tell newcomers to a culture what kinds of people are most likely to advance quickly in the organization and what traits the culture most values. They are the subject of the stories members tell about appropriate behavior. Heroes don't need ceremonies or trophies to affect the culture. They just need to be believed.

Heroes may be people who have dedicated their lives to serving the organization or who have gone the extra mile for the group—a custodian who reads to students, for example, or a teacher who stops an intruder.

To have a hero, it helps to have a villain. Some heroes may have fought a common enemy in the past, such as by standing up to unpopular policies or curricular changes. Cultures need villains to help clarify what is most important; they become stronger when their members can band together in the face of a threat. Some villains can even be manufactured by leaders if they feel as though more cohesiveness is needed. *Villains can be anyone or anything that does not align with the values and beliefs of the culture.*

Values and Beliefs

Values are simply the things that we believe to be most important. Most values in schools are learned; over time, people may learn to value football, the marching band, or faculty meetings over other activities. Values are broad tendencies to prefer certain things over others, and thus help members prioritize aspects of their lives. In education, we often speak of "putting the child first." Schools that don't do this will behave differently than those that do.

The stories we tell and the symbols we use let those inside and outside of the culture know what we value most.

Values provide the basis for a system of beliefs, which are "learned responses to threats made on the institution" that "exert a powerful influence over what people think" (Kuh & Whitt, 1988, p. 25). Beliefs allow us to subconsciously determine how to perceive reality. Because beliefs can be hard to explain, groups use concrete examples such as artifacts, stories, or symbols to let outsiders know what they are. The stories we tell and the symbols we use let those inside and outside of the culture know what we value most. Schein (1992) notes that "the most effective means for leaders to embed particular values and beliefs into the daily life of an organization are: what they pay attention to and reward, the ways they allocate resources, role modeling, how they deal with critical events, and through the criteria used to hire, promote, and terminate staff" (Schein, 1992, p. 252).

A culture is built around values, which are manifested in behaviors. A change in behaviors might be attributable to a change in the culture if it is a behavior that persists over time and if it occurs regardless of who is watching. Many scholars of culture believe that attempting to change a culture is extremely difficult, if not impossible, and that leaders actually hope to change *behaviors* in the hope that this will help to shift the culture as well.

Subcultures

We all belong to more than one group at the same time and unavoidably carry several layers of mental programming within us that reflect the values of each group. We tend to behave as we're expected to by other members of each group. Here are some well-established groups that we tend to divide ourselves into and that can have a major influence on how we act:

- Country, state, or region
- Religion
- Gender
- Age or generation
- Ethnicity or cultural heritage

- Social class
- Sports-team fandom
- Type of car we drive
- Genre of books or movies we like
- Favorite writers or artists
- Types of exercise we enjoy
- Type of computer we use
- Type of military experience
- Specific schools we've attended
- Social media websites we use

Can you picture how members of each of the above groups tend to behave? When you're a member of a group, it can be hard to see the stereotypes associated with it, though it's often quite easy for outsiders (e.g., Europeans might find Americans overly friendly and informal; PC users might think of Mac users as artsy or pretentious). Subcultures find ways to make their members feel a sense of solidarity with each other and a degree of wariness toward outsiders.

We usually determine which of the subcultures to which we belong influence the way we act the most, though we can shift when the values of our preferred subculture clash with those of another. (A member of a motorcycle gang who also attends church every Sunday will probably act differently when alone with his biker pals than he does among his fellow congregants, for example.)

In schools, we may find subcultures to be manifestations of the structures already in place—of departments or grade levels; or of veteran teachers rallying to protect a dying culture from a new one; or of teachers who are counting down to retirement.

There are many reasons that subcultures may develop, and leaders would be wasting time to try and stop them from developing. However, they may consider trying to influence people to join subcultures that may fit preferred behaviors better or have a more positive influence on a desired vision.

Sometimes a subculture will embrace the true essence of the leadership's vision for the school. If such a group exists or can be made to exist in a school, then leaders have a microcosm of the school culture eager to fulfill its demands. Some subcultures may even be making decisions about the future of the school independent of school leadership—such groups may be able to influence others in the school.

Sometimes a subculture will embrace the true essence of the leadership's vision for the school.

Just like larger cultures, subcultures are not inherently positive or negative. It really just depends on whether they decide to use their powers for good or ill. Although they may not always contribute to a feeling of community within the parent culture, they can offer individuals the rewards they need that they may not be able to get from the larger culture alone (Kuh & Whitt, 1988).

Subcultures may form when a subgroup responds differently to a situation than do others in the larger group. For example, in a school that has decided to adopt block scheduling, some teachers might band together to oppose the idea. (After a while, that same subgroup might find itself a conduit for opposing additional matters related to school operations— to the point that what once reflected the pushback of a few naysaying teachers could blossom into a full-scale civil war among faculty if leadership doesn't step in.) Another example: A group of teachers particularly enamored with new technology might take risks on emerging innovations and, eventually, provide effective support and valuable training for colleagues.

Just about every culture is a subculture of a larger culture. According to Van Maanen and Barley (1985), true subcultures must meet the following criteria:

- Regular interaction among members
- Group self-consciousness
- Shared problems
- Action based on distinct collective understandings

The actions of a strong subculture can evolve over time into norms that will differ from those of both the main culture and of other subcultures (Horowitz, 1987), but could come back to influence the parent culture.

In schools, the building-level culture is the parent culture to the subcultures (or cliques) that exist. If routine patterns of behavior within one group are considered normal, different activities performed by another subgroup may be judged abnormal by the parent culture (Morgan, 1986, as cited in Kuh & Whitt). For example, if the parent culture does not effectively celebrate student success, staff may look down upon colleagues in any subculture that attempts to do so.

In every school, it is important to identify the subculture that seems to wield the most power. If school leaders acknowledge such groups, they can recruit them to persuade the larger faculty to accept changes in the way things are done. However, if leaders ignore such groups, then there's a chance that they can "go rogue" and voice their opposition to the leadership's vision among colleagues. It's in a school's best interests for the best teachers in the building—the ones with the best track record at yielding academic success from students—to be afforded the opportunity to come together and provide some informal leadership for the school. Otherwise, the stories, symbols, heroes, and rituals of the school will risk supporting something other than the school's core purpose: student learning.

In every school, it is important to identify the subculture that seems to wield the most power.

Schein (1992) suggests that subcultures can develop alternate modes of thinking—what he calls parallel learning systems—that can decrease anxiety among members as changes are gradually introduced into the larger system, noting that "trial and error in the temporary parallel system can create the necessary psychological safety needed" for school-wide change to occur (p. 317). The best way to change the larger school culture, then, could very well be to empower a powerful subculture. (Of course, if the empowered subculture is made up of ineffective teachers, the parent culture could actually become worse rather than better.)

Subcultures give us permission to do (or not do) the right thing. Our closest cohorts can either support positive goals or enable negative behaviors. As Jim Rohn puts it, "You are the average of the five people you spend the most time with" (Rohn, n.d.).

CHAPTER 4

What Type of Culture
Do You Want?

It's easy, but misleading, to compare one school's culture to another's. This is not a beauty contest, and cultures are not best assessed using normative analyses. There's no one-size-fits-all recipe for ensuring a positive school culture—no two settings have the same particular mix of students, parents, teachers, support staff, physical location, and community—but there are identifiable ingredients that the most effective cultures have in common.

As you walk down the hall, look into classrooms, stand in the lunchroom, and watch students arrive and leave school each day, what type of behaviors do you see that seem to define these moments? What patterns recur that make your school unique? How might a visitor describe what he or she sees? As discussed in the previous chapter, day-to-day behaviors provide a sense of normalcy to those who work at and attend a school—a sense of *who they are*—and affirmation that things are working just fine. These routines are the culture's way of asking you to leave it alone.

The real challenge is to be able to observe our surroundings without being influenced by the cultural filters that we adopt over time. These filters can make us find a justification for everything (negative) in our school—misbehaving students, frustrated teachers, trash on the floor. The school culture impresses on us that such conditions are not only acceptable, but define us.

How a Vision of the Future Can Help You Change the Culture

Are there aspects of what you see, hear, and feel in your school that you would like to change? Not all behaviors are culturally ingrained. In fact, there are some that we can change by simply asking people to behave differently—particularly if they themselves wish, deep down, to change. Other behaviors may actually be deep seated and rooted in the culture's traditions or norms. Imagine yourself walking through your school five months or even five years from now to see students acting out, teachers fed up, and papers littering the halls. Would you think that any of these conditions were part of a vision and largely influenced by the school's culture?

A vision of the future is not simply a generic statement of positivity—it reflects a capacity to imagine a new reality and to understand all the components necessary to achieve and maintain it. Most of those components are people: imperfect humans with biases, preferences, habits, insecurities, superstitions, families, faiths, priorities, and values that may or may not all be for the best—*because the culture, whether positive or negative, has told them what "best" means.*

When you think about your school, remember that *something* is driving the individuals in it to act as they do. It may not be something that the leadership can control at this time. Maybe it's simply due to an outdated mentality that a few veteran teachers have perpetuated.

It helps to know who in your school has a vision for the school's future. There will always be a few people who do (as well as a few determined to keep the status quo). In fact, some are implementing their plans as you read this.

Types of School Cultures

For our purposes, we'll be discussing six general types of school cultures in this book. The first five were introduced by Fullan and Hargreaves (1996), and the sixth by Deal and Kennedy (1999):

1. Collaborative,
2. Comfortable-Collaborative,
3. Contrived-Collegial,
4. Balkanized,
5. Fragmented, and
6. Toxic.

Of course, these are only general types—the complexity of school cultures means that these sorts of categories are necessarily simplifications.

School Culture Type 1:
The Collaborative School Culture

This is the theoretical nirvana of school cultures—one that embraces learning for all adults and students. In a collaborative school culture, teachers share strong educational values, work together to pursue professional development opportunities, and are committed to improving their work. They are aggressively curious about teaching and learning. For the most part, their discussions focus on student achievement, and they spend time observing each other to critically analyze teaching methods. School leaders in a collaborative culture are adamant about challenging ineffective teaching practices while at the same time encouraging teachers' individual development. Research confirms that a collaborative school culture correlates positively with student achievement (Gruenert, 2005). In fact, the term "collaborative culture" is shorthand for all the good things that schools should be doing. Help, support, trust, openness, collective reflection, and collective efficacy are at the heart of a collaborative culture.

"When we speak of changing schools into more collaborative organizations, what we really mean is that we want to change the nature of the relationships, or patterns of relating"

As Pounder (1998) notes, "When we speak of changing schools into more collaborative organizations, what we really mean is that we want to change the nature of the relationships, or patterns of relating" (p. 29). Collaborating with colleagues grants us "access to expanded knowledge, resources, and creative alternatives for action" (p. 90)—and also reveals any latent weaknesses in our methodology. Of course, as in any culture, a collaborative one will have its share of personnel issues and other problems that are hard to resolve, but it is the optimal framework for resolving them. Regardless of how intense a problem is, the culture itself supports those who are trying to make the best decisions.

A collaborative culture feels a bit like family: Although individuals may not always get along, they will support each other when push comes to shove. A collaborative culture is a strong culture in which most people are on the same page. It would take a major crisis to put a dent in it.

School Culture Type 2: Comfortable-Collaborative

This is the type of culture many schools tend to believe that they have, and they could well be correct—it's a very common type. Schools have always been polite places; they're where most of us learn to get along and fit in with others. As students, we are forced to share space and work in small groups with people we may not like or have much in common with. In so doing, we learn the value of cooperation, courtesy, and compliance. Teachers expect students to be nice to each other, and principals expect teachers to do the same.

Being nice to each other is generally a good idea, but it can inhibit the practice of providing feedback in the form of criticism or even an alternative viewpoint. Many teachers will hesitate to voice their disagreement with one another for fear of hurting someone's feelings. In the comfortable school culture, it is more important to get along than to teach effectively.

Teachers in a comfortable-collaborative school culture don't ask essential questions about their work and how to improve;

they limit their conversations to sharing advice and tricks of the trade. In this type of culture, it is important for all teachers to be happy and satisfied with their work, but also to save any deep reflection that might get them to the next level for when they aren't busy (i.e., never).

Being nice to each other is generally a good idea, but it can inhibit the practice of providing feedback in the form of criticism or even an alternative viewpoint.

In a comfortable-collaborative school culture, teachers are generally aware of what their colleagues are doing in their classrooms, and they occasionally visit each other to discuss successes, but conversations about challenging students don't drill down very deep so as not to expose a teacher's weakness. Though teachers might share on how best to help at-risk students, they tread lightly for fear of indicting their peers' methods. The motto of a comfortable-collaborative school culture could be, "We are all fighting the same battle, so we need to get along."

A comfortable-collaborative school culture is not compatible with true collaboration if teachers are so comfortable that they don't wish to get better at what they do—what Dweck (2007) calls a fixed mindset. Teachers may not want to try anything different in order to avoid compromising future praise. This may be typical in high-performing schools wary of risking a dip in student achievement. Extrinsic rewards supplant intrinsic motivation in a comfortable school culture. Teachers begin looking for reasons other than a moral imperative to keep working hard (Sergiovanni, 1990). The intrinsic fires that burn in first-year teachers need to be reignited if a school is to break out of its comfortable rut. This effort needs to be led by the principal and rewarded by the culture. In the same way that good is the enemy of great (Collins, 2001), comfortable is the enemy of true collaboration.

School Culture Type 3: Contrived-Collegial

Let's be upfront: Any leader trying to shape a new culture in his or her school will necessarily introduce policies or strategies that feel forced or smack of micro-managing to teachers. School cultures can't improve without purposeful leadership; they can only become better *at protecting themselves*. When a principal becomes aware that his or her school culture isn't as supportive of learning as it could be, whatever he or she does to change things will be taken by some as a threat to their belief systems and to the school's very identity.

In a contrived-collegial school culture, leadership determines how staff are to behave. Often, principals will attempt to speed up the process of school improvement by enforcing collaboration and controlling the situations that foster it. As teacher behaviors become more and more regulated, teacher autonomy is diminished. Though the contrived-collegial school culture is meant to support new approaches and techniques to teaching, it can feel superficial and actually reduce teachers' motivation to cooperate with any changes. Such a culture may initially discourage true collegiality by forcing relationships among teachers who might not otherwise collaborate. Leadership will expect teachers to meet and discuss the progress of student achievement, then file a report to prove that they did so.

Any leader trying to shape a new culture in his or her school will necessarily introduce policies or strategies that feel forced or smack of micro-managing to teachers.

Although some contrivance is necessary for the development of a truly collaborative culture, knowing when to back off and let the seeds germinate can be challenging. The pace of cultural change is slow; people need time to process and reflect on what's new and attain a sense of ownership over it—jumping back into the driver's seat too soon can cause the shift to lose traction. To sell a new vision, it's best to wait for respected teachers to identify with it and put it in their own words. Teachers are likelier to emulate one another than to simply abide by what the principal says. Although it can be frustrating to contrive situations designed to build a new culture and then watch as nothing happens for a while, remember that culture resides in people's minds, so to expect an immediate shift in mindset is not realistic.

School Culture Type 4: Balkanized

If the fragmented culture encourages competition among individuals, a balkanized culture encourages it among small groups. In this type of culture, collaboration occurs only within cliques of like-minded staff. When the parent culture sets up teachers to compete against each other, subcultures can grow in strength for the wrong reason. Teachers who feel the need to compete for position, resources, and territory may recruit other teachers to join them in a clique. If there is a conflict between what the principal says to do and what the clique collectively says to do, the latter will tend to win out.

Members of a subculture will sit together at meetings, whispering, laughing, and bonding with each other. They will support each other when leadership creates stress by employing party-line decision making. Stronger groups know that they have the capacity to gang up on weaker ones to leverage behaviors. Staff in balkanized school cultures thus run the risk of being divided and lorded over by the stronger of many existing cliques.

School Culture Type 5: Fragmented

In this type of culture, people pretty much do their own thing. There usually isn't much drama because most simply don't care what others are doing. Staff are collegial and may share a laugh on occasion, but for the most part each has his or her own territory and likes it that way. Meetings may feel like meaningless rituals, with most teachers watching the clock so that they can get back to their silos. Classroom doors stay closed—both literally and figuratively. Successful teachers might attribute their effectiveness precisely to the autonomy that they are afforded by administrators.

A school with a fragmented culture may not exude a sense that anything is wrong. Teachers are friendly to each other in the halls; some might even eat lunch together. The problem with this type of culture is a lack of *professional* interaction among teachers, especially regarding best practices or student achievement.

There are many reasons a school culture may become fragmented. In the current era of accountability, it is easier for teachers to work independently. Merit pay discourages teachers from sharing their secrets of the craft. Teaching becomes a competition—and if teachers are competing, chances are they're having their students compete, too. In a fragmented culture, educating students is an "every-man-for-himself" proposition.

In a fragmented culture, educating students is an "every-man-for-himself" proposition.

Teachers in a fragmented school culture tend to enjoy some degree of insulation from interference from the community or central office. If staff could build a moat around the school, they would—and around each classroom. Such a culture fosters individualism at the expense of collaboration and external support. After all, collaboration can be a double-edged sword: As Pounder (1998) notes, "Schools collaborating with local businesses and corporations may find themselves somewhat dependent on and vulnerable to the scrutiny of these entities. Financial or other types of resources received from these businesses may place contingencies on the schools that administrators and teachers find unacceptable, yet shunning such support from key community members may set the school up for future conflicts."

The life of a principal is easy if you never open a classroom door. Because a fragmented culture is hands-off in this way, it attracts teachers who fear micromanaging principals. If your students are doing well, administrators leave you alone; if you have a problem, it's up to you to fix it. Asking for help is seen as a sign of weakness; providing help is a sign of arrogance. In a fragmented school culture, because teachers are usually unaware of what their colleagues are up to, they don't feel a stake in the success of all the school's students.

In a fragmented culture, nothing new is seriously considered because staff members are content with the status quo.

The interdependence of a collaborative culture can feel invasive to teachers in a fragmented culture, especially as it "often occurs at the expense of professional discretion" (Pounder, 1998, p. 29). Most teachers in a fragmented culture use professional discretion without much need for affirmation. Forcing a more collaborative culture on these teachers may be perceived as allowing others to intrude on this discretion.

In a fragmented culture, nothing new is seriously considered because staff members are content with the status quo, though they might discuss new teaching strategies and some might even experiment with them. Leaders in these schools are seldom available, and when they are, they may be little more than a smiling face rather than an educational resource. Some teachers might even view asking for the principal's help as the first step in creating a paper trail that could eventually get them fired.

School Culture Type 6: Toxic

If a collaborative culture is what all schools should strive for, a toxic culture is what they should try to avoid at all costs.

Think of a school where teachers do little more than sleep at their desks, hand out worksheets, humiliate students publicly, and gossip about colleagues. It only takes a few negative teachers for a culture to become toxic. Unfortunately, because of the power that a culture holds over the perceptions of its members, it can often be hard for teachers to see just how dysfunctional their school has become.

In a toxic culture, it isn't uncommon for teachers to focus on the negative aspects of the school's operations and personnel and even to use these flaws as a justification for poor performance. Just a few minor issues can give teachers permission to have low expectations of their students. What's more, this type of attitude does not feel particularly negative to the teacher, but necessary in the face of the school's problems. It also functions as a bonding mechanism for teachers.

A toxic culture may not be immediately evident to visitors because one of its hallmarks is the ability of staff to hide their beliefs.

A school with a toxic culture isn't necessarily an unhappy place. Staff might be very satisfied with their performance and will proudly say so. Toxic teachers can be very confident. In fact, they are sometimes the ones who speak the loudest, dress the most professionally, and have the tidiest classrooms. But when teachers in a toxic culture collaborate, their purpose for doing so might not align with the goal of fostering student achievement. Instead, their purpose may be simply to protect what they value: themselves. A toxic culture may not be immediately evident to visitors because one of its hallmarks is *the ability of staff to hide their beliefs.* Any guided tour of a school with a toxic culture may not reveal much of what's really going on behind the curtain. If an outsider does spot something toxic, staff can usually explain it away—"Though the teachers may *seem* rude, we regard their tough attitudes as essential to the services we offer." To the staff of a school with a toxic culture, the outsider simply doesn't understand what it takes to run the school given the types of students they have to deal with and the lack of support they receive.

Not all teachers in a toxic school culture will share the toxic mindset, but a significant proportion will. A new teacher seeking to fit in, or a frustrated teacher lacking administrative support, or a teacher counting down to retirement, can willfully ignore the toxic culture. In some schools, staff will closely scrutinize any efforts teachers expend toward student success—what is best for students takes a backseat to what is best for teachers. A toxic culture may start as a subculture of a few negative teachers and evolve over time into a decision-making force.

A toxic culture can function as a self-fulfilling prophecy: As teachers prioritize survival over improvement, they lower their regard for students. Some may even purposely act in a manner that makes students want to avoid them, such as by using ridicule, sarcasm, and humiliation in the classroom. And if even a few students do better than expected in this type of culture, they'll be held up as examples in support of a belief system that perpetuates toxic teacher behaviors. Toxic teachers will always be able to find someone in the classroom and community who adores them.

Teachers or students who've never experienced a more positive culture will come to think of a toxic one as normal. To them, this is what school is supposed to be; if students want to succeed, they need to embrace the same negative values that the teachers do. Parents who grew up in a toxic school culture will glorify it and push their children to appreciate it. To folks like these, anyone who tries to change the school's culture just doesn't understand what's best for the kids involved. In some schools and communities, it's almost a badge of pride to take a class with a particularly negative teacher—like a fraternity initiation or a tradition passed down through generations.

A toxic school culture expends energy on preventing change. Past failures resurface regularly as proof that resistance to change is a sign of strength, confidence, and competence. Administrators might maintain the toxicity by keeping lines of communication directive and one-way. The culture becomes stronger and more homogeneous over time as good teachers escape to more positive environments. There is a pervasive sense of hopelessness and pessimism among those who remain and aspire to improve. Ceremonies to celebrate student successes seem phony and become a point of contention and ridicule. Teachers live for the weekend and count down to the next holiday because they'd rather be anywhere else than helping students at the school.

A toxic school culture expends energy on preventing change.

In a toxic school culture, ineffective or negative teachers can be perceived as heroes by colleagues with the same mindset if they blame students' parents or the administration for their own failings. By talking the same language and validating other teachers' woes, they can become very powerful people, rallying the troops against the enemy—in this case, personal responsibility. Avoidance of responsibility is one reason that many ineffective teachers shy away from professional development and even social media: they don't want to see evidence of success elsewhere, because then their excuses might not hold up.

* * *

Chances are that your school fits one or more of the school-culture types discussed in this chapter, though one type is likely to predominate. As you were reading, we hope that you pictured some of the faces in your building and are starting to consider strategies for shaping a new and improved culture at your school. What might be a clue that things are actually changing? When is it time to reapply pressure? How much pressure do you need to apply? What might change look like *in your school?*

CHAPTER 5

What Type of Culture Do You Have?

*K*nowing the type of school culture you *have* will help you to plan for the one you *want*. One way to learn more about your school culture is by completing the Culture Typology Activity developed by Gruenert and Valentine (2006; see Figure 5.1). This activity basically immerses you in the nuances of your school culture and requires you to determine the degree to which you observe and participate in certain behaviors. The activity does not ask you to judge your school culture; it simply allows you to inventory the actions at your school. Nor does it provide definitive results—it is designed as a conversation-starter and -sustainer for school leaders trying to reveal their current cultural type and gain insights as to what their desired culture might look like.

12 Aspects of School Culture

The first column of Figure 5.1 presents key aspects of a school culture. By reviewing and honestly assessing the degree to which each exists in your school, you can get some idea as to the type of school culture you have. Here's a brief rundown of each aspect, followed by questions to consider when assessing each one.

Student Achievement

All teachers will talk about how well their students are doing in class. Some are very detail-oriented, providing play-by-play

Fig 5.1 School Culture Typology Activity

	TOXIC	FRAGMENTED	BALKANIZED	CONTRIVED COLLEGIAL	COMFORTABLE COLLABORATIVE	COLLABORATIVE
STUDENT ACHIEVEMENT	___ Many teachers believe that if students fail it is the students' fault	___ Teachers usually do not discuss issues related to student achievement	___ Most teacher discussions related to student achievement are restricted to within departments, cliques, or close friends	___ Teachers are given time to discuss student achievement and are expected to use it for that purpose	___ Teachers are given time to discuss student achievement but spend most of this time giving one another advice	___ Teachers are given time to discuss student achievement and spend this time critically analyzing one another's practice
COLLEGIAL AWARENESS	___ Many teachers do not care about the effectiveness of other teachers	___ Most of the teachers are unaware of what other teachers are teaching	___ Most teachers are aware of only what their friends in the school are teaching	___ School leaders expect teachers to know what their colleagues are teaching	___ Teachers occasionally observe and discuss what their colleagues are teaching	___ Teachers seek out opportunities to observe and discuss what other teachers are teaching
SHARED VALUES	___ Values that many teachers share don't fit students' needs	___ There is not much agreement among teachers concerning educational values	___ There are small groups of teachers who share educational values	___ School leaders provide teachers with a list of school values	___ Teachers generally agree on educational values	___ Teachers strongly agree on educational values
DECISION MAKING	___ Decisions are easily made because many teachers don't care what happens	___ Teachers are usually not interested in participating in decisions that concern students	___ There are small groups of teachers who attempt to control all decisions concerning students	___ School leaders expect teachers to participate in all decisions concerning students	___ Teachers occasionally show an interest in decisions made concerning students	___ Teachers are expected to participate in decisions concerning students

(continued)

Fig 5.1 School Culture Typology Activity (*continued*)

	TOXIC	FRAGMENTED	BALKANIZED	CONTRIVED COLLEGIAL	COMFORTABLE COLLABORATIVE	COLLABORATIVE
RISK TAKING	___ Many teachers protect their teaching styles from "innovation"	___ Most teachers typically do not experiment with new ideas	___ Innovations are usually initiated within a single grade or department	___ School leaders mandate that teachers try new ideas	___ Teachers occasionally like to experiment with new ideas	___ Teachers are constantly looking for new ideas
TRUST	___ Teachers talk behind their colleagues' backs	___ Trust among teachers is not considered necessary	___ There are teachers who only trust certain colleagues	___ Teachers are placed in situations where they are required to trust each other	___ Trust among teachers is assumed and not a critical issue	___ There is strong interdependence among teachers
OPENNESS	___ Teachers who are committed to students and to learning are subject to criticism	___ Teachers usually are not interested in suggestions concerning instruction made by other teachers	___ Teachers usually keep their opinions about instruction among their friends	___ Teachers are expected to contribute to discussions about effective teaching at meetings	___ Teachers are occasionally open to giving or receiving advice concerning instruction	___ Teachers are very interested in their colleagues' opinions concerning instruction
PARENT RELATIONS	___ Many teachers avoid parents whenever possible	___ Teachers would rather not have parents' input regarding instructional practice	___ There are cliques of teachers that parents perceive as superior to others	___ School leaders require teachers to be in contact with parents regularly	___ Most teachers are comfortable when parents want to be involved in instructional practices	___ Teachers aggressively seek the involvement of parents in classroom instruction

	Column A	Column B	Column C	Column D	Column E	Column F
LEADERSHIP	___ School leaders are seen as obstacles to growth and development	___ School leaders are not very visible in the school	___ School leaders frequently visit or praise the same teachers	___ School leaders monitor teacher collaboration	___ School leaders encourage teachers to give each other advice without being too critical	___ School leaders challenge ineffective teaching and encourage teachers to do the same
COMMUNICATION	___ School policies seem to inhibit teachers' abilities to discuss student achievement	___ Communication among teachers is not considered important	___ It is difficult to have productive dialogue with certain groups of teachers	___ Communication is dominated by top-down mandates	___ Warm and fuzzy conversations permeate the school	___ Any teacher can talk to any other teacher about teaching practice
SOCIALIZATION	___ New teachers are quickly indoctrinated by negative staff members	___ Teachers quickly learn that the school has an "every man for himself" culture	___ New teachers are informally labeled, then typecast as belonging to certain teacher cliques	___ There are many mandatory meetings for new teachers to attend	___ New teachers are encouraged to share their experiences with other faculty members	___ All teachers assume some responsibility for helping new teachers adjust
ORGANIZATION HISTORY	___ Teachers are quick to share negative stories about the school	___ "Teachers asking for help" has traditionally been considered a professional weakness	___ Some grades, departments, or teams consider their successes as separate from the whole school	___ School leaders have established strong control over much of what goes on at school	___ The school is known for its constant celebrations	___ There is an understanding that school improvement is a continuous issue
TOTAL:	Column A:___	Column B:___	Column C:___	Column D:___	Column E:___	Column F:___

of everything their students do; others might just say that their students are doing okay and leave it at that. In your school, to what degree do teachers substantively discuss student achievement? Do these discussions challenge teachers to reflect on and possibly reevaluate their practice?

Collegial Awareness

It's important to know how much teachers in your school believe they can learn from colleagues—not only by talking, but also by actually watching each other teach. Teachers often complain that it's hard to find time for scheduling classroom observations, and that even when they do, the observations don't yield much beneficial information. If a school culture encourages teachers to believe that they can improve their own practice by watching their colleagues in action, we believe that teachers will find time to do it. In your school, how much time do teachers invest in observing one another for the purpose of improving their practice?

Shared Values

School leaders need to know how strong their school culture is. When the teachers at a school are all in agreement about the building's educational values, they are not able to hide what they do because the culture itself, in the form of their peers, will hold them accountable. In this setting, no evaluation instrument or administrative threat will carry the same weight as the opinions of one's colleagues. In your school, to what degree are teachers on the same page regarding educational values?

Decision Making

This element taps into the theme of intrinsic motivation. We believe that when teachers feel they are making a professional contribution to their school, they enjoy their work more and accomplish far more than what any merit pay can yield. Teachers in an effective school culture expect to be included in most decisions related to student success. In your school, to what degree do teachers value the opportunity to participate in making decisions that affect student achievement?

When teachers feel they are making a professional contribution to their school, they enjoy their work more and accomplish far more than what any merit pay can yield.

Risk Taking

Some teachers are perpetually engaged in mini action-research projects as they seek to improve their craft; others believe that they learned everything they need to know about teaching as they went through the K–12 system themselves. We believe that effective school cultures encourage instructional experiments and teachers sharing their results, whether at faculty meetings or in the parking lot. In your school, to what degree do teachers value the opportunity to experiment with new ideas in the classroom?

Trust

Trust is such a complex concept that we could write a whole book on that one topic alone. In the context of school culture, what we mean is an interdependence that boasts, "We've got one another's backs." In an effective culture, members are confident that they can share their professional struggles with anyone else in the culture without invaliding their work. In your school, to what degree do faculty members exhibit trust in one another?

Openness

Assessment of this element can reveal whether a culture is merely comfortable or truly collaborative. Though professional learning communities are great for sharing craft knowledge, only in the most effective cultures do teachers feel free to

---

Assessment of openness can reveal whether a culture is merely comfortable or truly collaborative.

---

critique one another and to grow from the experience. In your school, if one teacher is observing another in the classroom, would he or she feel free to offer constructive criticism?

Parent Relations

Some schools welcome parents' contributions more than others. The most effective school cultures find ways to involve even the meanest or most apathetic parents; teachers have permission, written or unwritten, to initiate parent engagement by any means that works. Leaving a voice mail for parents is not enough in a truly effective culture—teachers need to be proactive when they contact parents and maintain positive relationships with all of them. Those who are uncomfortable with this process are expected to ask colleagues for advice. In your school, to what degree are parents valued for contributing to the educational process?

Leadership

By leadership here we refer specifically to the principal and leadership team most responsible for overall school improvement. In your school, how much does the leadership contribute to or hinder instructional improvement? Does the culture embrace opportunities to include school leaders, or does it encourage teachers to hide from them?

Communication

This aspect refers to conversations among teachers and between teachers and principals. Depending on the school culture, such conversations can be frequent and voluntary or rare and mandated; merely congenial or genuinely productive. In your school, to what degree do written or unwritten rules and expectations regulate communication among staff?

Socialization

The induction process is more structured at some schools than others. Some simply hand a new teacher the keys to his or her classroom and say "Good luck"; others may have a veteran teacher waiting to begin the mentoring process on a teacher's first day. The best school cultures ensure that new teachers spend a lot of time with the best teachers in the building and discourage new recruits from spending too much time around less effective teachers who might indoctrinate them with poor habits. In your school, to what degree do effective faculty support the induction of new teachers?

Organizational History

Cultures try to build a present based on what has happened in the past. Even the best schools promote a nostalgic view of how they became effective. Schools glorify names and events from the past through memorials, awards, and plaques, but mostly through stories. In your school, how do past events and long-gone members of the school community influence the present and future?

Using the School Culture Typology Activity

The descriptors in the far-right column of the School Culture Typology Activity, under Collaborative, explain what you might expect each of the elements discussed in this chapter to look like under ideal conditions—these are the targets that you'll want to aim for. You may need to reinterpret the descriptors to some degree so that they better fit the specifics of your particular school culture. For example, the descriptor "Teachers have conversations about student achievement" can refer to many different types of conversations. If the conversations are engrained in the culture, they will occur more often informally than formally. (If you specifically ask faculty *not* to discuss student achievement and they do it anyway, that's a sure sign that the conversations are indeed a part of the culture.)

Though it's rare for a school culture to be predominantly toxic, it doesn't take very many teachers or incidents for a school to lean in that direction.

Conversely, the descriptors in the far-left column, under Toxic, seem almost comical. Though it's rare for a school culture to be predominantly toxic, it doesn't take very many teachers or incidents for a school to lean in that direction, especially if it has a weak culture (that is, one in which the teachers aren't all on the same page). Behaviors common to a toxic culture are detrimental to student learning.

Here's the protocol: Ask teachers at your school to complete the School Culture Typology Activity by determining, on a scale of 0 to 10, the degree to which the descriptor in each cell reflects behaviors in your school. If the behavior described in the cell occurs all the time at your school, it gets 10 points; if it is unheard of, it gets a 0. When the numbers are added up, each row should have a total of 10 points. Once every cell is accounted for, have teachers add up the totals for each of the six columns. The column with the most points represents the culture that each teacher believes the school is closest to.

This activity can be administered to teachers in large-group, small-group, or individual settings. Obviously, the less trust there is among faculty members, the harder it will be to collect data in an open forum. Be sure to honor requests for anonymity. Ideally, a staff member who is considered neutral by most staff will be assigned to collect and tally the results.

The data from this activity will provide your faculty with much to contemplate. High numbers in the first three left-hand columns suggest that your school's culture is on the wrong track, whereas high numbers in the last three right-hand columns suggest the opposite. It is important that no individual is singled out as being responsible for any results, and that no one department or clique is demonized by the larger group.

The goal of this activity is to determine what type of culture you have and how far you are from the one that you want. Seems simple enough, but it isn't. The real conversations start when you ask faculty these follow-up questions:

- Do you feel that these results are accurate?
- How did we get to this place?
- Do we want to change? If so, how?
- What do we want to look like in five years?
- Do the target descriptors in the Collaborative column seem achievable?

- What first steps can we take to improve our school culture?

As with many research instruments, the School Culture Typology Activity is a means for determining both a school's baseline (its current condition) and necessary treatment (what we try to do to improve the current condition). The activity can also be used to determine whether the school culture has shifted over time by readministering it at a later date and comparing the original baseline with more current results.

When we talk about a school's culture, we are entering a sensitive zone. Questioning what has been done in the past will cause some teachers to feel uncomfortable. This is the culture pushing back, whispering in teachers' ears, "Everything we do around here works fine, don't do anything different." We are not trying to discredit the past—staff did the best they could with what they had—we just don't want an ineffective past to shape the future. The formal and informal conversations that occur because of this activity will provide a framework for future planning.

When sharing the results of the activity, point to any strengths as reasons why the school is doing well, and any weaknesses as reasons why it will be difficult for things to get better. The more a group doubts the purpose of its traditions, rituals, and ceremonies, the weaker its current culture will become—and the current culture will not change until it becomes weaker.

CHAPTER 6

The School Culture Survey

*A*s we've noted, a collaborative school culture provides the ideal setting for student learning. It's also a setting in which teachers learn from each other as much as they do from other sources. It would be difficult to argue against the notion of teachers learning from one another as a strategy for improving a school. The challenge for school leaders is getting the school culture to embrace this approach. One way to address the challenge is to determine just how collaborative your school currently is. That is the goal of the School Culture Survey (SCS) developed by Steve Gruenert (one of the authors of this book) and Jerry Valentine, both of the Middle Level Leadership Center. The survey is shown in Figure 6.1.

The School Culture Survey is an instrument designed to be administered to teachers in a school building to get a sense of how much their school culture is collaborative. We use the term *collaborative* to mean much more than simply teachers working with other teachers—in this case we also mean the existence of trust, peer observations, a compelling mission, and so on.

The SCS helps us to inventory the behaviors typical of a collaborative school culture. It also provides a baseline for school leaders who wish to shape a new school culture, just as the School Culture Typology Activity does. As leaders begin to implement change in the school, the SCS can be readministrated to

Fig 6.1 The School Culture Survey

Directions: Please indicate the degree to which each statement describes conditions in your school using the following scale:

1=Strongly Disagree   2=Disagree   3=Undecided   4=Agree   5=Strongly Agree

	1	2	3	4	5
1. Teachers utilize professional networks to obtain information and resources for classroom instruction.					
2. Leaders value teachers' ideas.					
3. Teachers have opportunities for dialogue and planning across grades and subjects.					
4. Teachers trust each other.					
5. Teachers support the mission of the school.					
6. Teachers and parents have common expectations for student performance.					
7. Leaders in the school trust the professional judgments of teachers.					
8. Teachers spend considerable time planning together.					
9. Teachers regularly seek ideas from seminars, colleagues, and conferences.					
10. Teachers are willing to help out whenever there is a problem.					
11. Leaders take time to praise teachers who perform well.					

(continued)

Fig 6.1 The School Culture Survey (*continued*)

1=Strongly Disagree   2=Disagree   3=Undecided   4=Agree   5=Strongly Agree

	1	2	3	4	5
12. The school mission provides a clear sense of direction for teachers.					
13. Parents trust teachers' professional judgments.					
14. Teachers are involved in the decision-making process.					
15. Teachers take time to observe each other teaching.					
16. Professional development is valued by the faculty.					
17. Teachers' ideas are valued by other teachers.					
18. Leaders in the school facilitate teachers working together.					
19. Teachers understand the mission of the school.					
20. Teachers are kept informed on current issues in the school.					
21. Teachers and parents communicate frequently about student performance.					
22. Teacher involvement in policy or decision making is taken seriously.					
23. Teachers are generally aware of what other teachers are teaching.					
24. Teachers maintain a current knowledge base about the learning process.					

	1=Strongly Disagree 2=Disagree 3=Undecided 4=Agree 5=Strongly Agree	1	2	3	4	5
25.	Teachers work cooperatively in groups.					
26.	Teachers are rewarded for experimenting with new ideas and techniques.					
27.	The school mission statement reflects the values of the community.					
28.	Leaders support risk taking and innovation in teaching.					
29.	Teachers work together to develop and evaluate programs and projects.					
30.	The faculty values school improvement.					
31.	Teaching performance reflects the mission of the school.					
32.	Administrators protect instruction and planning time.					
33.	Disagreements over instructional practice are voiced openly and discussed.					
34.	Teachers are encouraged to share ideas.					
35.	Students generally accept responsibility for their schooling, for example by being mentally engaged in class and completing homework assignments.					

determine whether or not (and to what degree) the culture is shifting to a more collaborative posture.

The SCS has strong reliability—that is, teachers are likely to interpret the survey items in a similar way. We achieve high reliability by using statistical analyses. When we analyzed the different factors represented by the survey, we found that the 35 survey items could be divided into six main categories:

1. Collaborative Leadership: Items in this category measure the degree to which school leaders establish, maintain, and support collaborative relationships with and among school staff.

Target behaviors: Leaders value teachers' ideas, seek input from teachers, engage teachers in decision making, trust teachers' professional judgment, support and reward risk taking and innovative ideas designed to improve student achievement, and reinforce the sharing of ideas and effective practices among all staff.

SCS items in this category: 2, 7, 11, 14, 18, 20, 22, 26, 28, 32, 34

2. Teacher Collaboration: Items in this category measure the degree to which teachers engage in constructive dialogue that furthers the educational vision of the school.

Target behaviors: Teachers across the school plan together, observe and discuss teaching practices, evaluate programs, and develop an awareness of the practices and programs of other teachers.

SCS items in this category: 3, 8, 15, 23, 29, 33

3. Professional Development: Items in this category measure the degree to which teachers value continuous personal development and schoolwide improvement.

Target behaviors: Teachers seek ideas from seminars, colleagues, organizations, and other professional sources to maintain current knowledge related to instructional practices.

SCS items in this category: 1, 9, 16, 24, 30

4. Unity of Purpose: Items in this category measure the degree to which teachers work toward a common mission for the school.

Target behaviors: Teachers understand, support, and perform in accordance with the school's mission.

SCS items in this category: 5, 12, 19, 27, 31

5. Collegial Support: Items in this category measure the degree to which teachers work together effectively.

Target behaviors: Teachers trust each other, value each other's ideas, and assist each other as they work to further the school's goals.

SCS items in this category: 4, 10, 17, 25

6. Learning Partnership: Items in this category measure the degree to which teachers, parents, and students work together for the common good of students.

Target behaviors: Parents and teachers share common expectations and communicate frequently about student performance, parents trust teachers, and students generally accept responsibility for their schooling.

SCS items in this category: 6, 13, 21, 35

What to Do with the Data

You will probably be drawn to the items that receive the lowest and highest scores on the survey, which makes sense. Just be sure not to ask for the scores of other schools; whatever they are doing is irrelevant to your school's culture. A good approach is to ask who "owns" each item—is it the domain of teachers or administrators? You can do this on your own or in a group. Then, ask whether you believe that the item represents something you *can* do, *might* be able to do, *doubt* you can do, or *can't possibly* do. For each item, ask why this is the case or not.

Because this is a survey about school culture, remember to think of the responses as those of the culture rather than of any one individual.

Because this is a survey about school culture, remember to think of the responses as those of the culture—a community voice—rather than of any one individual. It might seem weird, but if we act as if the culture is a living, thinking organism instead of simply background music, we will approach it with greater respect and caution.

As you identify the highest- and lowest-rated items in the survey, look for natural breaks. For example, let's say the highest-rated items have scores of 4.6, 4.5, 4.5, 4.4, and 4.1; in such a case, you'll want to cluster the first four scores together and focus on those. Though this isn't a particularly scientific way to approach analyzing survey results, it is practical.

When considering the highest-rated items in the survey, ask, "What is it in our culture that allows us to score highly on these?" If many of the highest-rated items are clustered in one of the six categories discussed earlier in this chapter, then your school is especially strong in that category.

By considering the standard deviation (SD) for each item, you can get an idea of how much teachers agreed on each one. An SD of around .60 or lower implies that most teachers were on the same page about the item. A higher SD suggests that they're not, and that the item may actually be a source of conflict among faculty. Here's where it gets interesting: A high SD suggests that there is an expert on that item in your building who has not yet had a voice in the matter.

Here's an example of what we mean. Imagine that the item "Teachers and parents have common expectations for student performance" has a particularly high SD. Such a point spread would imply that some teachers don't believe this to be true while others—perhaps teachers who have actually worked to make it so—believe that it is. Now imagine getting teachers with different opinions on the matter together to discuss it, maybe at a faculty meeting. In a collaborative culture, teachers would feel compelled to discuss the matter without prodding, and would be aggressive about finding a way to ensure that teachers and parents have common expectations.

Protocols for Using the Survey Data

One of the developers of the SCS, Jerry Valentine of the Middle Level Leadership Center, has been using the survey for many years and created the following protocols for faculty review of the resulting data:

1. Teachers split into groups of six per table, making sure that each group has a mix of teachers from different departments, grade levels, and subcultures. Each group receives the same printout of SCS data showing the scores for each item and for each of the six categories.
2. Each group ranks the six categories from high to low on a piece of chart paper, writing the mean scores for each next to each one. Everyone at the table should be able to view the same visual of the information at the same time.
3. Group members discuss among themselves whether or not they think the scores accurately reflect the school's culture.
4. Group members review the 35 survey items and list the 5 highest-rated and 5 lowest-rated items on separate sheets of chart paper.
5. Group members discuss among themselves whether or not they think the scores for the 10 selected items reflect the school's culture. They also discuss the categories that the items represent and consider whether particular categories are represented more than others.
6. If faculty previously completed the School Culture Typology Activity, group members review the findings from the activity and discuss whether or not they align with the SCS data.

7. On a sheet of chart paper, the group lists what it considers to be the four or five most pressing concerns regarding the school's culture. On a separate sheet, the group then lists one or two practical strategies that might address each of these concerns.

8. One at a time, groups share the concerns they came up with and the practical strategies for addressing each one.

**

The School Culture Typology Activity and the School Culture Survey can be used together to give you a better understanding of your school's culture. Each of these instruments can reinforce the data from the other. Whereas the SCS may be better for establishing baseline data, the School Culture Typology Activity might be more sensitive in picking up subtle changes early in the change process.

The trick for school leaders is in understanding how any item from either instrument can exist in unique ways at their school. Trust among teachers, for example, can take different forms. Getting teachers to trust one another in a culture that doesn't place value on it can be challenging. Doing it wrong—such as by proclaiming from the top of a desk that you are going to change the culture—will only make things worse.

Another challenge to bear in mind is that teacher self-reporting may or may not be precise. Will teachers respond honestly, or will they feel coerced to respond in a way that makes the school culture look good? Is it possible that a few negative teachers might skew results to make the school culture look bad? It's important to consider these questions whenever examining data related to people's perceptions. Still, if we can get a good response rate—50 percent or better—then we can usually trust the results.

CHAPTER 7

To Reveal the Invisible
and Start Conversations

*A*s you think about ways to reveal your school's culture and potentially expose issues that may be inhibiting student achievement, consider using the activities in this chapter.

Survey on the Purpose of Education

Without consensus among staff regarding the school's mission, improvement efforts may drift around a few common assumptions rather than strong, shared principles. Do we force children to attend school so they can become financially independent, or to pass tests? To shape their thinking into conformity, or to free their thinking and creativity? The answers to these questions are the foundation on which everything we do in schools should be built. Though consensus among school staff and community members is important, consensus among teachers is crucial. The survey shown in Figure 7.1 will allow you to assess the degree to which the teachers at your school are on the same page regarding the school's mission.

Thoughts to consider when using this instrument:

- Agreement among teachers is more important than identifying the right answer.
- Purpose is equal to mission—if we change the mission, then we also change the vision.

Fig 7.1 Survey on the Purpose of Education: Why Are We Here?

Directions: On a scale of 1 to 5, consider the degree you believe each of the following items constitutes a reason for providing an education in our society.

1=Strongly Disagree   2=Disagree   3=Undecided   4=Agree   5=Strongly Agree

	1	2	3	4	5
1. To teach students how to beat the system					
2. To learn the value of cooperation over competition					
3. To reduce the threat of global terrorism					
4. To help students become great at one thing					
5. To narrow the gap between the rich and the poor					
6. To learn how unfair the world is					
7. To learn the basics of academia (math, reading, science, history)					
8. To maintain world domination					
9. To make mistakes					
10. To recognize and resist unethical domestic/business practices					

(continued)

Fig 7.1 Survey on the Purpose of Education: Why Are We Here? *(continued)*

1=Strongly Disagree   2=Disagree   3=Undecided   4=Agree   5=Strongly Agree

	1	2	3	4	5
11. To pass tests					
12. To evolve into a less violent society					
13. To have fun					
14. To reduce environmental degradation					
15. To appreciate and aspire toward a professional disposition					
16. To use force prudently					
17. To increase one's sense of civic responsibility					
18. To become rich and independent					
19. To learn how to use credit					
20. To be a nice person					
21. To know how to use spare time					
22. To make more sense out of life					
23. To be trusting and trustworthy					

- Are the items that are easiest to measure at the top of everyone's list?
- Does the school "own" all of the items?
- The degree to which teachers agree on the importance of the items may provide a clue as to how strong your school's culture is. (Again: by "strong" we mean "difficult to change.")

Discussing the purpose of education can take a long time and require several meetings. People usually do not think about the purpose of education much, but when asked about it they can engage in deep philosophical discussions, even within themselves. To make this activity more relevant to your particular school, consider adding items to the bottom of the survey that reflect more local issues or issues that your school is especially focused on. Here are some examples:

- to continue the tradition of having a winning football team
- to keep the community from becoming consolidated
- to break the chain of poverty
- to support the local military base

People usually do not think about the purpose of education much, but when asked about it they can engage in deep philosophical discussions.

Local issues will define the culture of the community, of which the school is a subculture. Perhaps there is a specific issue in the community that is influencing the school's ability to improve. Most meetings would go faster if someone were always there to ask, "Why are we here?"

Elements of Culture Form

Though there is no definitive list of the elements that make up a culture—there may be hundreds of them—the form shown in Figure 7.2 considers 12 elements that are common to school cultures specifically. School leaders might leverage these elements when thinking about cultural change.

Fig 7.2 The Elements of Organizational Culture

VISION (what do people look forward to)	MISSION (why are we here)
RITUALS (habitual activities)	LANGUAGE (local jargon, humor)
CEREMONIES (glorified rituals)	SYMBOL (tangible stuff)
VALUES & BELIEFS (what's really important)	HERO (who are we proud of)
CLIMATE (the mood we are usually in)	NORMS (unwritten rules)
TOOLS (what we use to get work done)	STORY (myths passed on to rookies)

The Elements of Culture form will help to reveal your school's current culture. It may shed some light on some silly, innocuous behaviors; whether it sheds light on any dysfunction in the school will depend on how forthcoming teachers are in their responses. When completing the form, teachers should avoid pointing fingers at any one individual. This is an audit of the culture as a whole—if only one person is displaying a particular behavior, then that behavior is probably not part of the culture.

Your school culture is bound to be composed of more than 12 essential ingredients. The purpose of this form, however, is to reveal how your school's staff delivers information, solves problems, and protects its members. As with many of the activities offered in this book, the form does not provide a definitive outcome as much as help you to better understand both the concept of culture and the specific culture of your school.

Protocols for Completing the Form

It's best for teachers to complete the form when they are all in the same room and divided into small groups. The groups should represent a mix of different teacher subcultures within the school. Ask each group to consider examples of how each of the concepts in the form is made manifest at your school. Here are some examples:

- *Vision:* People around here look forward to Friday.
- *Routines:* We take attendance every hour in every class.
- *Norms:* Most teachers arrive at school around 7 a.m.
- *Values:* We value having clean rooms every morning.

When the groups are done filling out their forms, have them report out what they wrote, one element at a time. Use chart paper or an overhead projector to record the information for everyone to see. As the elements are recorded, patterns may emerge and themes may seem to develop. We are not judging any behaviors at this time; we are only building a list.

A good way to take this activity to the next level would be to ask whether the items within the elements listed serve or detract from the school's mission or vision. (Without a vision in place, this can be a difficult discussion.) Ask the teachers, "Is this who we are? Is this who we want to be?"

The "Who Owns What?" Survey

Student achievement, the dress code, attendance, even hygiene: Do you think students, teachers, and parents all agree on who is most responsible for each of these components? Should your teachers "own" everything? We think you would be surprised to find out how much students think *they're* responsible for.

Teachers will typically take ownership of grading and attendance; students will typically take ownership of how they dress for school; administrators will typically take ownership of maintaining the school's daily operations; parents will typically take ownership of ensuring that their kids get enough sleep each night. However, it's also possible that some of the individuals in your school community are not taking ownership of components that everyone assumes is theirs to own.

We codeveloped the survey shown in Figure 7.3 with a high school principal, Chris Mauk of Vigo County School

Fig 7.3 The "Who Owns What?" Survey

Directions: Given the following situations, determine who should have the most responsibility for it by placing a number 1 in that box. The second most responsible person will get a 2, third gets a 3, and the one least responsible gets a 4.

S=student P=parent T=teacher A=administrator	S	P	T	A
1. Student tardy for school.				
2. Student tardy for class.				
3. Students bullied at school often.				
4. Homework not getting finished.				
5. Learning in the classroom.				
6. Student with poor hygiene.				
7. Enforcing school dress code.				
8. Most students failing a test in one class.				
9. Student performance on state-standardized tests.				
10. Care and maintenance of school property.				
11. Warm/welcoming school.				
12. Teacher attitudes toward students.				
13. Teacher morale.				
14. Repeated misbehavior by students.				
15. Student attendance rates.				
16. Students' desire to come to school.				
17. Teachers' desire to come to school.				
18. Parent involvement/concern/support.				
19. Ensuring conditions for student success.				
20. Graduation rates.				

Corporation in Indiana, who was struggling to get adults in his school community to take ownership of certain behaviors in their culture. The ultimate goal of the survey is to reveal the beliefs that frame behaviors within the culture. This is a big first step in gaining a better understanding of the culture (Deal & Peterson, 2009).

We distributed the survey to 500 students from four different schools and asked them to determine who in their school community was responsible for each of the items listed. The tabulated results can be seen in Figure 7.4. As you review the results shown in the table, you will notice that the behaviors with the smallest mean values (in gray) are those that students most perceive as the responsibility of the group named at the top of the column. This means that students believe that the group in question has the capacity to change the identified behavior. The table also shows standard deviations (SD) for each item— the smaller the SD, the more students agreed on who is responsible for the behavior.

The table in Figure 7.4 shows that students believe they themselves should be primarily responsible for the following six behaviors listed in the survey:

- Student tardy for school.
- Student tardy for class.
- Homework not getting finished.
- Repeated misbehavior by students.
- Students' desire to come to school.
- Student with poor hygiene. (This one was a tie, with parents also largely considered responsible.)

Fig 7.4 Results from Survey Data (*n* = 476)

Survey Item	Admin. Mean	Admin. SD	Parent Mean	Parent SD	Student Mean	Student SD	Teacher Mean	Teacher SD
Student tardy for school.	3.51	.732	1.67	.754	1.62	.731	3.20	.656
Student tardy for class.	3.28	.902	2.54	1.010	1.40	.843	2.84	.767
Students bullied at school often.	2.21	1.167	3.02	.881	2.72	1.265	2.08	.897
Homework not getting finished.	3.72	.709	2.22	.682	1.25	.718	2.83	.595
Learning in the classroom.	2.95	.921	3.30	.853	2.02	.965	1.63	.850
Student with poor hygiene.	3.60	.753	1.64	.712	1.64	.770	3.11	.709
Enforcing school dress code.	2.27	1.285	2.45	.937	2.79	1.244	2.47	.952
Most students failing a test in one class.	2.95	1.088	3.01	.893	2.05	1.112	1.90	.988
Student performance on state-standardized tests.	2.86	1.083	3.16	.852	2.06	1.157	1.87	.884
Care and maintenance of school property.	1.59	.938	3.59	.730	2.56	1.063	2.22	.726
Warm/welcoming school.	1.40	.802	3.53	.754	2.87	.892	2.02	.688
Teacher attitudes toward students.	2.45	.977	3.29	.900	2.57	1.082	1.65	.996
Teacher morale.	2.28	1.036	3.24	.875	2.39	1.160	2.09	1.130
Repeated misbehavior by students.	3.11	1.079	2.49	.971	1.76	1.134	2.50	.901
Student attendance rates.	3.27	.989	1.76	.904	1.83	.912	2.81	.920
Students' desire to come to school.	2.94	1.195	2.54	1.008	2.15	1.207	2.28	.992
Teachers' desire to come to school.	2.12	.915	3.28	.902	2.53	1.083	2.02	1.174
Parent involvement/concern/support.	2.78	1.048	1.75	1.088	2.93	1.142	2.27	.842
Ensuring conditions for student success.	2.33	1.136	2.53	.989	2.90	1.236	1.75	.847
Graduation rates.	2.58	1.185	2.63	1.070	2.11	1.245	2.02	.862

Do any of these results seem counterintuitive to you? Do you think that knowing this information might change the way a teacher approaches his or her day? To what degree do you think that teachers would agree with the students' responses? Imagine the discussions that teachers might have with students after reviewing the survey results. How might a positive teacher respond? What about a negative teacher? Revealing the gap between what students think and what teachers think can provide insight as to the behaviors of both groups—especially their behaviors when the other group is watching. And yet, if you don't have a truly collaborative school culture, these issues are all but undiscussable (Argyris, 2010).

There are many ways to administer this survey. In the pilot program, we asked teachers to administer it to their students while they were in the room. The completed surveys were then collected, placed in an envelope, and returned to us for analysis. During a Back to School retreat, teachers were asked to respond to survey items themselves before learning the student results. To get the full benefit of this exercise, we recommend having a sample of parents and administrators provide their responses to the survey.

If your school culture allows for it, a faculty meeting devoted to teacher debate over the results might be worth considering. We see the survey as a great opportunity for teachers to collaboratively discuss best practices. It might be interesting to readminister the survey at the end of the school year to see if anything has changed.

Grade level may influence the survey responses. Take the item "Students tardy for school," for example: High school students will obviously be better equipped to control this behavior than elementary students. But disparities among students are beside the point: The real purpose of the exercise is to illuminate the differences in perception between students and teachers and the ways in which the school culture might contribute to those differences. Most teachers believe

---

The real purpose of the exercise is to illuminate the differences in perception between students and teachers and the ways in which the school culture might contribute to those differences.

---

that they themselves are responsible for student learning, such as by setting the conditions for it to happen, whereas students "own" their homework and classroom behavior—but each group owns its desire to come to school, regardless of what the other group thinks. Dweck (2007) refers to this attitude as a *learning mindset;* it is typically shared from one generation to the next.

The most useful aspect of using the "Who Owns What?" survey is the discussion after it's been completed, whether that's between faculty and students, among teachers only, or between teachers and administrators. A collaborative school culture will welcome these discussions; a toxic school culture will deflect them or even misrepresent the survey results.

Implications

Dysfunction in schools can often be traced to a lack of ownership of certain actions. If everyone believes that someone else is in charge of an action, then that action will never happen. Although most teachers are given job descriptions that delineate the actions for which they're responsible, those job descriptions are, like speed-limit signs, often ignored. Peer pressure and informal inductions by colleagues are more likely to dictate what teachers believe their responsibilities are than whatever is written in the job description. This is the culture at work. Remember: The culture will always support "the way we do things around here."

It's not the survey results that will change teachers' mindsets regarding ownership of behaviors, it's their emotional responses to those results (Keyton, 2005). When we have a learning mindset (Dweck, 2007), we control how we behave and we are eager to improve. By contrast, when we have a fixed mindset, we let the culture do the thinking for us. It's easy to picture teachers becoming incensed at the students' responses—"How dare these kids tell me what my job is!"—so instead of throwing the survey results in teachers' faces, provide them with a forum for having deep discussions about the data. This is an opportunity to let effective teachers teach their ineffective colleagues what is most important—despite what those ineffective teachers may want to do or what has happened in the past.

School leaders can't just wave a magic wand and expect teachers to shift their values and beliefs instantly. Change of that sort is an evolving process that begins with an awareness that something just isn't right. Perhaps this activity can help jump-start that awareness.

Exposing the beliefs of an organization's members can be a sensitive proposition. Individuals may espouse beliefs that they've never acted upon or deny their true beliefs; their beliefs may also be tied to a subculture. Strong allegiance to the wrong subculture could sabotage cultural rewiring. This activity can help teachers see how their beliefs may be inhibiting student achievement and, hopefully, help them to close the gap between "how we do things around here" and best practices.

You can make the survey even more powerful by asking teachers to add any items missing from it that they feel are very important to their school. You may also want to give the students, parents, and administrators a chance to provide their input as well. Comparing and contrasting the findings from different groups might help each group see where the differences lie—differences that may well be roadblocks to improvement.

The most important aspect of professional development in any school is the dialogue that teachers engage in afterward. If teachers aren't afforded the opportunity to reflect on professional development with their colleagues, they will have learned a limited amount from any exercise. The activities in this book are specifically designed to stimulate conversations among teachers—a critical component of a collaborative school culture. They are not intended to form a part of any evaluation; they are ways of assessing where we are and where we want to be as a school, not necessarily as individuals.

CHAPTER 8

The Beat Goes On— or Does It?

*H*opefully you have not jumped to this chapter too quickly! Many school leaders believe they already understand certain concepts when they really don't and will begin to tinker with them before they're ready. Ethnographers typically believe that cultural change will never quite live up to expectations, humans being as imperfect as they are. Others who study leadership believe that cultural change is always a slow process, a bit like evolution, taking as much as 5 to 15 years to accomplish (Schein, 1992; Wagner, 1994). Still others believe that cultural change can be expedited through purposeful leadership. However long change takes, no one should be dissuaded from taking the first steps toward improvement. Whether or not the change occurs quickly and is maintained will depend on the strength of the preexisting culture and the knowledge and skills that school leaders bring to the table.

"Culture is a holistic, context-bound, and subjective set of attitudes, values, assumptions, and beliefs . . . what people attend to and how they interpret actions and events are filtered through lenses colored by past experiences" (Kuh & Whitt, 1988, p. 95). Because subcultures ensure that multiple realities exist in any school, managerial control of the culture—that is, the extent to which school leaders can intentionally change cultural properties—is bound to be quite limited (Kuh & Whitt, 1988). When pursuing cultural change, leaders shouldn't consider changing the culture entirely—even in the most toxic school cultures, some aspects are probably functioning quite well. School leaders need to understand the specific aspects of the culture that are interfering with the school's goals.

Which stories do you want to repeat? Which ones do you need to adapt? Which ones do you want to get rid of? What do you need to change? What do you need to leave alone? Hopefully, the activities discussed in the previous chapters have caused you to think about these questions.

When pursuing cultural change, we need to make sure that we always protect the most valuable people in the organization. Unfortunately, it isn't always clear who those people are. It's possible to be both successful within the culture and ineffective as a teacher—the culture may applaud those whose behaviors align perfectly with the unwritten rules, regardless of their professional competency.

When pursuing cultural change, we need to make sure that we always protect the most valuable people in the organization.

Moving the Process Forward

Can we really change what people believe? The perception that culture can be intentionally controlled does violence to some important properties of culture, such as its complex, holistic character (Geertz, 1973, as cited in Kuh & Whitt, 1988).

Though Schein (1992) notes that cultural "changes require anywhere from 5–15 or more years if basic assumptions are really to be changed without destroying and rebuilding the organization" (p. 317), once the changes begin, things can move pretty fast.

Heifetz, Grashow, and Linsky (2009) note that "some people who rise to the top of an organization due to their ability to work within the rules, written and unwritten, of the system will have little interest in challenging the structures, culture, or defaults that define that system especially for those in mid-career who have been enjoying professional success" (p. 52). It seems some do not want the next generation to have it any easier than they did.

It is interesting to study sports teams through the filter of culture. Despite having the same coach and player turnover rates, some teams seem to win consistently while others appear constantly stuck in a quagmire of mediocrity. However, every once in a great, great while, the pattern is disrupted.

For example, consider the Boston Red Sox, a team that had about a century of struggles. Year after year, decade after decade, the team was unable to break what seemed to be a curse. Then somehow, out of nowhere, the Red Sox rallied back from a 0–3 deficit against the Yankees (their archenemy) and, finally, made it to the 2004 World Series, where they swept four games and won the championship. And this wasn't just a one-year blip—the Red Sox have had continued success since then, even winning the championship again in 2007 and 2013. We don't pretend to know baseball well enough to be able to explain what accounts for the team's improvement, but we do think it's a good example of how success is possible even when it seems like it isn't. Determining what's wrong with your culture is the key to improving it. Doing this as efficiently as possible may be challenging, but it's necessary. Culture is not some mystical power that thrives on superstition; the locus of control is within the scope of leadership.

Culture is not some mystical power that thrives on superstition; the locus of control is within the scope of leadership.

The Jump Start

Rather than wait for the Good Witch Glenda to intervene, school leaders should look for aspects of their culture that they can influence if they want to significantly increase the odds of cultural improvement. And improvement is never completely impossible—after all, if you put enough monkeys in a room with enough typewriters, don't they eventually come up with the Constitution (or, at least, a CliffsNotes version)?

Perhaps a lot of your students live in poverty; maybe you get little to no central-office support. There's no question that such factors make rewiring your culture a challenge. And yet, somewhere a school with the same demographics or level of support has made great strides and is even winning awards. If that school can do it, yours can, too—you just need to figure out how in the face of a culture always ready to tell you that you can't. The following strategies can help you to jump-start the rewiring process.

Jump-Start Strategy 1: Stop with the Excuses

Stopping with the excuses is a good place to start. There are teachers in your school or district who can have a positive effect on all students and build good relations with their parents. There are also those who can't do either. Teachers in the latter camp hope desperately that something out of their control is keeping them from helping students do well in school—it's because the parents don't care, or last year's teacher wasn't good enough, or there's not enough administrative support. But those teachers have colleagues in the same school who are facing the same challenges and don't fire off excuses—they just find ways to be successful. What accounts for these two very different approaches? Maybe it's the tale of two subcultures with very different belief systems. In a collaborative culture, the successful teachers would be encouraged to share their approach with other teachers. Unfortunately, this doesn't happen in most schools.

School leaders need to encourage others to stop looking for reasons not to accomplish things. But first they have to make sure that they aren't looking for excuses either. Rather than focus on roadblocks to advancement, find the people in your school who have overcome those roadblocks and learn from them. Never lose sight of how often change starts with a small group of people. Determining when something moves from climate to culture isn't nearly as essential as building a positive culture that lasts.

Jump-Start Strategy 2: Stop Generalizing

All parents are not mean, and "kids nowadays" are not all the same. It is vital to be cautious when discussing the contributions that different groups of people have made to a culture, lest you begin to take generalizations at face value. When talking about how your school's culture came to be, take pains to highlight the positive contributions that different stakeholders have made.

Leaders will, of course, want to seek input and guidance from the best, most caring teachers as they make decisions. However, there may be times when ineffective or disengaged teachers can provide direction as well. For example, if you toss out an idea at a staff meeting and one of your least effective teachers immediately agrees with it, this might be a signal that you ought to rethink the idea.

Jump-Start Strategy 3:
Introduce a New Enemy to the Group

This is a risky one, but it can work. Share a story of someone who is challenging some of the group's less effective behaviors. A common enemy will bring a group together quicker than anything—just don't let that enemy be you!

Jump-Start Strategy 4:
Let the Most Effective Teachers in on the Skinny

If you let the teachers with the most positive influence in your school know that you're embarking on a journey to transform your school's culture, they will probably show their gratitude for making them insiders by taking the project of cultural change to a level you never imagined. Be careful not to foment conflict when doing this—after all, the teachers who represent the future of your school need to bring those who represent the past into the future with them.

The Culture as a Family

Do you remember sitting around the dinner table with your family growing up? In many families, there is an expectation as to where everyone should sit, whether it's verbally acknowledged or not. Sitting down to eat becomes a well-established routine, perhaps a ritual—or even, on holidays, a ceremony. After all, a family is a fairly small group of people, all of whom have roles and "scripts" that they've been following over many years. The family culture is strongly defined. As in most cultures, one or two people have a particularly strong influence on the actions of the rest of the group. No one dares sit in their seats—this is culture whispering in the ears of its members.

How does the family culture react if a guest comes over for dinner one night? People will often move from their accustomed seats to accommodate the guest—everyone except for the one or two "power players" with the most influence. Family members will also tend to behave a little differently around their guest. These shifts in the dinner dynamic last only as long as the guest is around—they are changes in the climate, not the culture.

Now, what if the family has a long-term houseguest? Not just any houseguest, but, let's say, a favorite aunt. (Not the one who needs a shave, thank goodness—the one that everyone actually likes.) What if, on her very first night at dinner, Aunt Millie sits in one of the power players' seats—the dad's, let's say? The first instinct of family members might be to gasp in disbelief or ask her to move. But this isn't one of their smelly cousins—it's their very favorite aunt! So what do the family members do? They accommodate her. Why? Because they revere her; they hold her in such high regard that even a power player relocates for her. Aunt Millie may even have intentionally taken the power player's seat to help improve the dynamics at the table.

As in most cultures, one or two people have a particularly strong influence on the actions of the rest of the group.

Everyone is on their best behavior during dinner—the climate is positive. Pleasant conversation is had and people say "please" and "thank you" as they pass each other servings of food. Then, right at the start of dessert, Aunt Millie makes a statement: "I love this family so much, yet I hardly ever get to see you! Each night while I'm here, why don't we take dessert as an opportunity for each of us to share three things that happened to us during the day? This would help me get to know what your lives are like."

The rest of the family responds with awkward silence. Everyone but Aunt Millie looks down and refuses to make eye contact.

Having anticipated this reaction, Aunt Millie asks if it would be OK for her to go first. At that, the others at the table smile in relief and nod their approval.

Aunt Millie starts off with a self-deprecating story about getting lost on her way to the store—she took all sorts of silly wrong turns before finally finding it, and then couldn't find her way home! As she laughs at her own foibles, she brings a smile to everyone else's face. She's not done, though: After arriving home from the store, she realized that she had left her glasses there and headed back to get them—only to get lost again in the process! By now, everyone at the table is in stitches.

When her story is over, Aunt Millie pauses, takes a deep breath, and relates one more detail from her day. That afternoon, she says, her young nephew, who is also sitting at the table, brought her his favorite teddy bear. He told her that when he sleeps at a strange house, his teddy bear always comforts him, so he wants her to have it while she's here. At the table, Aunt Millie turns to her nephew and gives him a warm smile.

Everyone else at the table now takes a turn discussing the events of the day: someone threw up at school, traffic was really bad that morning—things of that nature. The whole family ends up having a lot of fun, thanks largely to Aunt Millie's example. On reflection, it occurs to some of those at the table that Aunt Millie went first for two reasons: to model how to share stories, and to give everyone else time to think. Maybe this consideration on her part is one reason she's everyone's favorite.

The next evening, Aunt Millie is the last to arrive at the dinner table. And what chair is left open for her? The one she sat in the night before—the power player's chair. She really *is* everyone's favorite aunt! As she takes her seat, Aunt Millie announces, "I can't wait until dessert to hear three things that happened during everyone's day!" She does this to remind everyone—that way they all have time to silently plan what they're going to share.

Because Aunt Millie knows that everyone needs more than just one day of modeling to catch on to the new routine, she asks if anyone would mind if she goes first again. Naturally, nobody does. Aunt Millie starts off with two lighthearted tales, then once more shares a story about someone else at the table: This time, the story is about Aunt Millie's niece, who brought her a favorite afghan to keep her warm at night. (After all, she had to do something to match her kiss-up brother!) Once again, everyone at the table proceeds to share a few things that happened during the day. Though they don't all get up to three stories, they all make an effort to participate.

On the third night at dinner, Aunt Millie once again announces that she can't wait to hear everyone's three stories. This time, someone chimes in, "Can I go first?" It's Aunt Millie's young nephew, who decides to share a story about her—how she packed him a peanut butter and jelly sandwich for lunch that day and included a note that said, "I cut it diagonally so that all of the flavor stays in." Mom, who grew up with Aunt Millie's sandwiches, reflects on the fact that she's always cut sandwiched diagonally for that very reason, having been taught by Aunt Millie to do so from a very young age.

Three weeks pass by, and it's time for Aunt Millie to be going. Everyone smothers her with hugs and kisses as she goes out the door. That night at dinner, Dad, now back in his usual seat, says, "Can I share my three things first tonight?"

And so a culture begins to shift.

CHAPTER 9

How Long Does It Take
to Rewire a Culture?

*H*ow long it takes to rewire a culture will depend largely on how long the culture has been established and how entrenched it is. As the story of Aunt Millie in Chapter 8 shows, a single individual with vision and drive who is held in high regard by members of the culture can hasten cultural change. In every case, however, the pace of cultural change is as unique as the culture itself.

The Challenging Class

Within every school, each classroom has a subculture of its own. As the school year progresses, each of these subcultures becomes more and more entrenched—for good or ill. And the more entrenched a culture is, the harder it is to change, particularly if the agent of change is to one degree or another subservient to it.

Imagine a teacher who struggles a lot with classroom management and has poor relations with students—someone whose class is basically out of control. Let's say that this teacher quits her job in the middle of the school year and is replaced by one of the most effective and well-liked teachers in the building. Within a week of the latter teacher's tenure at the head of the class, the classroom is bound to be completely transformed—as though the more effective teacher had been in charge all along. The highly effective teacher doesn't wait for his or her students to manifest poor behavior, and the students don't challenge the new teacher as much as they did the less effective one. Two different teachers, same students and school culture, totally different results.

Now let's imagine that the ineffective teacher is replaced by one who is somewhere in the middle—not totally ineffective, but not the most effective either. This type of teacher probably can't get every student to behave as well as the most effective teacher can. The class may be a bit more manageable than under the first teacher, but the average teacher's efforts are not enough to overcome a long-established classroom culture.

The most effective teacher succeeds by not letting the preexisting norms and expectations matter.

In the above examples, the most effective teacher succeeds by not letting the preexisting norms and expectations matter. Of course, classroom cultures will never be as strong as the school cultures of which they're a part—after all, they rarely extend beyond the school year, whereas school cultures evolve over many years. But the criteria for changing a school culture are the same as those for classrooms. In a toxic culture, an average leader will not be able to improve the culture alone; at best, he or she will encourage some teachers to consider new approaches, but will need a lot of tools and supporters to accomplish true change. It is unfortunate when there is an effective change agent in the building who has no voice in the professional development of his or her colleagues. Many school cultures will exert pressure on teachers to maintain their distance when helping other teachers.

Although the precise moment of a full cultural shift can be hard to discern, that it's actually happened usually isn't. We cannot time-stamp something as complex as cultural change, but we can certainly notice it. It's a bit like losing weight: If someone's been overweight for his or her entire life and gradually begins to shed pounds, the change can either be temporary (e.g., a

---

Although the precise moment of full cultural shift can be hard to discern, that it's actually happened usually isn't.

---

change in climate) or it may be a long-lasting reflection of a new lifestyle (e.g., a change in culture). For weight loss to stick, an individual needs to permanently change his or her belief system and approach toward physical health and requires the support of friends and colleagues.

Imagine a school that is trying to move its culture from one that makes decisions based on what's best for adults to one that makes decisions based on what's best for students. A change in lip service about the culture is pretty easy, but getting to real change is much more challenging. Reducing the amount of lecture time, introducing flipped-classroom instruction, and developing individualized lessons are all actions that may take a great deal of effort. The more the specifics of cultural change challenge the norms of a school, the more the preexisting culture will resist them.

Zero to Ten

Sometimes cultures are so entrenched that change for the better seems impossible. Cultural change is not an exact science; it is messy, unpredictable, and, often, uncomfortable. Taking risks, no matter how small, is essential to the process—sometimes, the biggest hurdle in trying to move from 0 to 10 is the step from 0 to 1. If you have 80 staff members, don't just focus on the ones who resist change the most. Every time you change someone's attitude toward change from negative to neutral or from neutral to positive, you are softening the culture up for more significant changes down the road.

Though there is no preset timeline for how long change should take, the journey itself can be quite rewarding—and the bigger the challenge, the more satisfying surmounting it becomes. To quote an old saying, "Sometimes it's more fun to mow when the grass is long."

CHAPTER 10

Breakthroughs

For real culture change to occur in any organization, there will need to be at least one or two individuals who are willing to be the first to make a move—leaders, in other words.

It Starts with One

There's no question that getting everyone in your school to shift beliefs and practices at the same time is a challenge. The existing culture is dead-set against dramatic changes, especially those that are implemented with a sense of urgency. To get the process moving, it's essential to find that first risk-taker frustrated enough with the status quo to begin the journey. This individual needs to be respected enough by his or her peers to attract them to the cause—if there's only one risk-taker in the school ready to make a change, he or she runs the risk of invalidating the new vision entirely with a single misstep. Cultural change must be a school-wide movement, not just an individual effort.

A Coach's Story

Imagine a high school where one of the cultural norms is that unless they're occupied with extracurriculars, all teachers are required to attend the monthly faculty meeting. Now let's say that this school hires a new football coach, and he decides to attend the first faculty meeting of the year. At the meeting, the teachers whisper and point the coach out to each other, but no one says anything to him.

Cultural change must be a school-wide movement, not just an individual effort.

The next day, the volleyball coach approaches the football coach. "Just so you know, us coaches don't have to attend those meetings," she says. "We have practice after school, so we're excused."

The football coach answers, "I've told my players that academics come first. If I really believe that, then I need to model it."

What's stronger in this case, the culture or the coach? One way to tell is by looking at how many of the other coaches at the school ended up following his lead. This particular example is actually a true story. By the end of the year, all the coaches in the school were making it a point to attend the faculty meetings.

The above example is a classic case of an accidental breakthrough. Though the volleyball coach nudged the football coach to conform to the cultural norms, the football coach refused—not out of a grand vision of cultural change, but out of his own personal convictions. If the principal had seen the football coach at the meeting and written him an appreciative note, the coach might have felt even more empowered to face any pushback from the culture.

Hiring for Rewiring

It's really nice when you can hire staff members who consistently do the right thing regardless of peer pressure, but people like that are few and far between. True risk-takers capable of breakthroughs are a rare breed—there are usually no more than a few in a school. These are the superstars who have the ability to do what is right while retaining the respect of their peers.

When hiring staff, look out for candidates who seem capable of intentionally contributing to cultural breakthroughs.

When hiring staff, look out for candidates who seem capable of intentionally contributing to cultural breakthroughs. For example, let's say you work at a school where teachers dress unprofessionally in class—an aspect of the culture that you'd like to bust. During the hiring interview, you might ask such questions as "How often would you wear a tie to school?" or "Do you think it's appropriate for teachers to wear jeans in the classroom?" both to identify candidates who are on the same page as you about the dress code and to let new hires know that this is an important issue for you. With these expectations in place, new teachers will be better prepared to confront any pressure from colleagues to conform to the unwanted cultural norm of unprofessional dress.

You may think that if you set new expectations, the teachers who meet them will be upset with the ones who don't. This may be true to some degree, but the teachers who meet expectations will be even more upset with you as their leader for letting their colleagues slack.

Consider the following example. At the first faculty meeting of the year, the school principal announces that he'd like all teachers to call parents and ask for their help before sending students to the office for misbehavior. A few weeks later, one teacher sends a student to the office for repeatedly not bringing a pencil to class without consulting the student's parents. In such a situation, if the principal wishes to retain credibility, he or she must intervene and discipline the teacher. Otherwise, the preexisting culture in which teachers aren't expected to call parents is affirmed.

Pooled Breakthroughs

Risk-takers are bound to be self-assured people—especially if they continue to flout negative cultural norms even in the face of blowback from colleagues. But even the most confident staff members will benefit from support. Pairing new staff members with veteran role models will positively influence both camps. Imagine if the football coach from our earlier example was asked to attend the monthly faculty meetings with a few assistant coaches—what a statement that would make!

We recently spent time at a school district where the coaches required their players to sit in the first three rows of all their classes (except when their seats are assigned), because research shows that students who sit in the front of the class perform better than those who sit in the back. The coaches in this school district model the behavior that they ask of their players by sitting in the first row at every staff meeting. When these cultural norms were introduced to the district, the dynamic of meetings quickly changed for the better—and because there were multiple risk-takers involved, over time the entrenched culture was less able to resist a breakthrough.

The Culture Follows the Teachers

When hiring new teachers, your goal is to have the existing culture bend toward the new teacher, not the other way around. This can be easier said than done, because a strong culture will necessarily resist any breakthroughs. To new staff members, the existing culture can be an alienating, ethnocentric force. If this is the case in your school, be sure to hire newcomers who will help bust it and give them the support they need. The same goes for staffing particular grade levels or departments—select those who will have the most effect on each discrete subculture.

When introducing new hires to the school community, you might want to let everyone know that they represent our best hope of getting where we want to be in five years. Some veteran teachers may not like this, but it's true—and it shows that you support the newcomers in the face of a resistant, entrenched culture. You will want to ensure that the first teachers the new hires meet—during summer orientation, for example—are also your strongest faculty members. This will probably require some behind-the-scenes coordination on your part. Remember: New teachers do not always know who the most toxic teachers are, and for their part, the most toxic teachers are usually looking for friends with whom to share their burdens.

Chances are that a new teacher is replacing someone else in the same role—a role that usually comes with a script that was last updated by the person being replaced. The more the new teacher sticks to the original script, the easier his or her transition into the role (and the culture) will be—don't let the new teacher assume the role of an ineffective teacher. And school leaders have control over this dynamic—after all, they provide the structures necessary for newcomers to assume identities that aren't chained to the past and that foster innovation.

New teachers must be given a voice and space to counter many pressures from the culture to prevent a breakthrough.

New teachers must be given a voice and space to counter many pressures from the culture to prevent a breakthrough. Yet at the same time they seek to be validated by their peers. What will this look like at your school?

CHAPTER 11

Leverage Points

*O*ne way to rewire your culture is by seeking out *points of least resistance* in your school—the *leverage points* at which the culture is (suddenly) made vulnerable to change. School crises provide leaders with an opportunity either to validate or to change the way the culture responds to certain situations. Implementation of outside mandates, electoral swings in school-board elections, construction work on the school campus—any number of events can be leveraged to introduce new ideas to the culture. For example, let's say that your school is in the process of implementing a new state-mandated teacher-evaluation system: This outside threat might strengthen bonds among faculty while also giving you, the school leader, an opening to address issues that may be holding the teachers back—and thus to rewire the culture.

Rituals and ceremonies that focus on the future, such as graduation celebrations, are great opportunities for introducing new ideas to the culture with minimal pushback. After all, when we think about the future, we do not defend the past as much.

According to Peterson and colleagues (1986), institutional cultures can be modified in the following seven ways:

1. By creating new units within the organization,
2. By changing personnel,

3. Through visionary leadership,
4. By redefining the mission,
5. By reorganizing the institution,
6. By using conflict to separate espoused from enacted values, and
7. By using crises to refocus goals and priorities. (p. 101)

Kuh and Whitt (1988), however, suggest that the empirical support for these findings points to changes in climate rather than culture, and we believe that their concerns have some merit.

Leverage Point:
The Start of the School Year

Picture the first day of school: students are dressed to impress, their supplies are neatly organized, and they're walking briskly from class to class. At the same time, they're often not yet sure where (or even who) their friends are. They don't yet know what to expect from their teachers. The year's subcultures haven't been established yet—anything, good or bad, is possible.

At the beginning of the year, the culture of each classroom is like a ball of clay waiting to be formed. Teachers' levels of engagement with students, their tone and manner, how they respond to student misbehavior—all of these elements and many others contribute to the ultimate shape of the culture. At the start of the school year, classrooms boast waxed floors, working pencil sharpeners, and full rolls of paper towels by the sink. The windows frame a freshly mowed lawn and a bunch of cheerful "Welcome Back!" signs.

Teachers walk into their first faculty meeting of the year with more of a spring in their step than they had the year before. They see new faces—colleagues they'd like to impress in the coming year; perhaps the room boasts a new coat of paint or new decorations along the bulletin boards. An air of hope and excitement prevails among all but the most jaded. If things were wonderful last year, everyone is proud of the school's achievements and ready to keep them up; if things weren't so great the year before, then staff may be determined to reverse the school's fortunes. No matter what the culture was like last year or even over the past 20 years, we now have the opportunity to change it—to make it *better*.

Though the start of the school year is just one of many possible leverage points on the academic calendar, it is the strongest, as it has the unique advantage of being preceded by the summer, which affords school leaders ample time to prepare.

Leverage Point: A New Principal

Deal and Peterson (2009) note that a culture is particularly vulnerable when a new leader shows up. Staff members are bound to compare a new principal to whoever previously held the post; it's up to the new recruit either to build on the successes of an effective predecessor or to move on from the disappointments of an ineffective one. The new principal's behavior in the first few hours, days, and weeks is pivotal—what he or she says and does will greatly affect the school community's expectations for the year.

Will the new principal roam the building with a clipboard and stopwatch, or will he or she mandate extra flextime for staff? Whether the vision is stricter or looser, chances are that employees will comply with it to some degree. The real challenge lies in inculcating the new vision in the culture.

Because staff members are usually on their very best behavior when they first meet the new principal, these moments could well be the softest leverage points for rewiring a school's culture. Of course, if you're the new principal, you must have both a vision and the skills to implement it. You also need to establish your preferences as soon as you can. For example, if on your first day at a new school the secretaries ask you how you'd like them to answer the phone, you should answer immediately and with specifics. By setting expectations early on, you avoid correcting behaviors down the line. Waiting until you admonish staff before revealing your preferences will cause staff to resent your actions and resist implementing your vision for the school. If this happens, it's you versus the culture—and the culture wins.

Changes in behavior show an effect on *climate*, not necessarily *culture*.

We're not saying that there isn't a place for correcting ineffective behaviors. It's just that changes in behavior show an effect on *climate*, not necessarily *culture*. Such changes can be fleeting if they're brought about by extrinsic motivation (for example, if they're actively enforced). True cultural transformation can't be bought—the school has to be ready for it. And the transformation will work best if you first develop one of the school's subcultures into a de facto leadership team.

Leverage Point: Natural Shifts in the Calendar Year

Every transition period in the school year is a natural point to leverage for rewiring your culture. Take, for example, New Year's: You could announce that your resolution for the coming year is to visit classrooms a lot more often so that you can observe all the wonderful things that the teachers are doing. You might even add that the students are bragging so much about their classes that you just can't wait to see what all the fuss is about.

What do you think will happen if you make this announcement? For a while, teachers might change the climate of their classrooms in anticipation of your arrival—cleaning up their rooms, tweaking their lessons, maybe even dressing more professionally. For this change in climate to become a change in culture, you must follow through on your promise and actually undertake frequent classroom observations. If you only visit a handful of teachers and leave it at that, the conspiracy theorists will have a field day: "Did he come to your room? He was in *mine,* I wonder why he wasn't in *yours*?" And if your visits are few and far between, you'll be greeted by suspicion— and a reluctance to accept a shift in the culture.

Another great time to leverage help from teachers is when you assign them their schedules. Communicate your draft schedule to the teachers; if any of them ask whether there's anything they can do in exchange for a more convenient schedule, reply that there is: They can help you to rewire the culture.

Leverage Point: The Holidays

Holiday assemblies and plays can encourage a spirit of good-will among staff—and when people are in good moods, they will receive proposed changes better. Use these occasions to plant a few seeds about any changes on the horizon. The holiday season is a great time to build up emotional credibility with staff. For example, consider sending parents holiday cards telling them how much their children matter to the school.

Leverage Point: Weddings and Funerals

Consider holding events outside of the school building to celebrate or mourn along with staff members during important moments in their lives. These are great times to connect more with others and possibly solidify your relationships.

Leverage Point: Awards and Recognitions

Use celebrations of awards and recognitions to rewire your school's culture. But be careful—jealousy can lead to award recipients being taken down a notch or two by colleagues. Such reactions can dissuade staff from working to shift the culture in the future.

Leverage Point: Test Scores

There are certain times of the year when educators' stomachs get tied up in knots in anticipation of student test scores. The effects of poor test scores on the culture can be negative or positive, depending on the actions that faculty take in response. If educators respond by blaming everything but themselves—last years' teachers, irresponsible parents, uninformed legislators—the culture will remain static. By contrast, if educators respond by critically examining their own behaviors, they may end up shifting the culture in a positive direction.

Positive scores may be due to teachers' efforts—or they could be due entirely to students' own talents. If scores are high, parents will naturally resist any changes to the culture. It's vital for educators to view positive scores as validation of their own hard work and to redouble any efforts aimed at improving achievement.

Leverage Point: Outside Directives

New testing guidelines, a different curricular focus, refinements to the teacher evaluation system—whatever the mandate, it doesn't usually take long for the effects to trickle—or slam—down onto schools. It's a good idea to intentionally use these mandates as a way of furthering culture change. In many schools, the first instinct of the culture is to fight any top-down directives. In these situations, many principals will try to reassure staff members that everything is going to be perfectly normal. But what if we do not want things to be normal? Don't we want to take advantage of the new mandates to do better than we've done before? Rather than reassure low-performing teachers in your school, make them aware of the opportunity that new mandates afford while also acknowledging the challenges they pose ("How are you going to deal with all of these changes?" "I bet you feel like you are in a tunnel and trains are coming from both directions!"). Don't let them settle back into their comfort zone of mediocrity.

Rewiring a culture is like turning around an ocean liner—it takes a long time.

Rewiring a culture is like turning around an ocean liner—it takes a long time. However, we don't want everyone in the school to change direction, as some are already pushing the culture ahead. These educators need reassuring in every way possible. But those who are working against progress should not be given the same degree of emotional support as those who are working for it unless they are willing to change direction. Of course, anytime teachers working against change choose to change their ways, leaders should be there to make the change easier for them.

Leverage Points: First- or One-Time Events

Culture uses the past as a template for the present. It is more important to the culture that responses to given situations be predictable rather than effective—after all, we can always make up excuses after the fact. However, when events occur

Culture uses the past as a template for the present.

for the first time, the culture has no template against which to compare the present. If approached carefully, these unsettled moments can serve as leverage points for rewiring your culture. Here are just a couple of examples.

Crises

We certainly hope your school never has to face a serious crisis such as a shooting or natural disaster, but if such an event does occur, it can offer an opening to change the culture for the better. However, as Pounder (1998) notes, "Threat and stress make people more determined to preserve their social structure and traditions" (p. 102).

The 1999 Columbine High School massacre and the terrorist attacks of September 11, 2001, caused many schools in the United States to reevaluate their approach to school safety, often by restricting visitor accessibility to students. How might the cultures of these schools differ from the culture of yours when it comes to, say, allowing students to have cell phones? At a local level, schools that have been hit by tornadoes or other natural disasters will tend to develop new ways to keep students safe when the weather turns foreboding. How might tornado drills make these school cultures differ from yours? Horrific events will change what people believe and alter the way they prepare for and react to similar events in the future. They also afford educators a unique opportunity to examine the importance of relationships in the school community and remind them of the essential roles that they play in the lives of others. Out of tragedy we can acquire a greater appreciation for life and how important it is to treat one other with the highest regard at all times.

The manner in which school staff deal with crises can create new norms that either support or challenge the culture's existing values. There are benefits for student achievement as well: "Crises heighten anxiety, and anxiety reduction is a powerful motivator of new learning. If people share intense emotional experiences and collectively learn how to reduce anxiety, they are more likely to remember what they have learned" (Schein, 1992, p. 237). Cultures teach their members how to cope with the problems that they collectively face, thus reducing the anxiety. It follows, then, that cultural change asks people to alter or even surrender their defense mechanisms.

Loss of Life

When facing the death of a colleague or student, the members of a school community will often rally together and end up developing a closeness with one another that may not have existed before. Life-changing events are good opportunities to reflect on how we live our lives and to consider what sort of legacy we are working to establish each day. The ultimate gift that others give us when they die is a recommitment to making a difference during our own time on earth.

Grants and Outside Recognition

Many schools pursue grants to fund cultural changes—new programs, additional resources, increased staffing, and so on—that often fail because they're being forced into a box that staff can't think outside of. And once the initiatives *do* fail, it doesn't take long for the culture to decide what to do with the grant money.

Pursuing grants and applying for awards in recognition of cultural changes are signs that a culture (or a culture-buster within it) is willing to risk the blow of being denied for the chance to be rewarded. Whether efforts are successful or not, these are opportunities for demonstrating what the culture values. And if efforts *are* successful, public celebrations of any successes are essential if those successes are to last. These celebrations are great occasions for culture-busters to share their efforts in pursuit of outside recognition with their colleagues and point out the positive effects that such recognition will have on the school. Though you might privately commend and provide extra support to the culture-busters who made the efforts and took the risks, you must ensure that a critical mass of staff feels invested in the change being rewarded.

CHAPTER 12

How the School-Year Cycle Affects Cultural Rewiring

*E*ducation is such an unusual profession: Every school year has a definitive starting point and a clear finish line. Leveraging this yearly cycle skillfully can be one of the most powerful ways to move your school's culture in a different direction. Usually, the beginning of the year is a time of renewed energy and hope, with teachers and support staff alike anticipating what's to come. Think about how lucky we are as educators to have these yearly opportunities to do better. Imagine a bank manager waking up one day in the fall and saying, "Things are going to be different around here this year!" It wouldn't quite work as well as it does for educators, would it?

The start of a new year offers both new and veteran staff members a chance to bond and possibly carry the torch for cultural change. During the summer break, physical improvements to the building might be undertaken that offer staff a renewed view of the school. Repainted rooms, new signage, decorations in the lunchroom—any of these kinds of physical changes can give staff a psychological jolt, telegraphing the idea that there's something new in the air. Sure, the complainers in the culture may whine that money is better spent on salary raises or technical upgrades, but the core of the faculty will likely appreciate positive tweaks to the environment.

So, what's the best way to use the academic calendar in the service of cultural change? Here are some tips and strategies for getting started.

The First Day

Find a few effective teachers in your organization whom you trust to help you with rewiring your culture. Share with them a few of your ideas for transforming the school, either one-on-one or in a group, but don't mention the word *culture*. Begin the conversations informally—you want staff to think of any changes as new ideas rather than initiatives. Talk about where your school currently is versus where you'd like it to be. Let teachers share their own ideas for a new direction in detail so that a collaborative vision of the future begins to take shape. Get teachers curious and excited about what's ahead. Consider sharing items from the surveys discussed in previous chapters to plant ideas in teachers' minds as to what you might want to achieve in the school. That should be enough for one day: Rather than overload staff with a flurry of small thoughts, focus on convincing them that positive change is possible and that they have the power to direct it.

Cultural shifts start off as concepts; it's only after a few years that these concepts will become entrenched.

Cultural shifts start off as concepts; it's only after a few years that these concepts will become entrenched—when teachers start meeting in hallways to discuss best practices, sharing their successes and frustrations in faculty meetings, observing one another at work in the classroom, and so on.

The First Week

Sustain the initial conversations from the first day throughout the week, informally. Discuss with your selected teachers how best to suggest new ideas to their colleagues. One approach might be to ask the selected teachers to start informal discussions with peers about a few new practices that they are thinking about implementing. In this way, you can indirectly help to guide the rewiring of teacher subcultures—especially as some teachers seek you out as they generate new ideas.

Give teachers permission to experiment with new approaches and encourage them to share their discoveries among themselves, perhaps during open discussion at a faculty meeting. Once the teachers have done this, talk to them about the concept of culture—and let *them* be the ones to bring the topic

---

Give teachers permission to experiment with new approaches and encourage them to share their discoveries among themselves.

---

to the rest of the school community. If you want to get something started, you must enlist the help of a few respected and connected teachers to sell it. People are much more likely to buy into ideas because their friends urge them to do so than simply because it is a good idea.

Thinking about the future is supposed to be fun, but the roadblocks we encounter when trying to get there are no fun at all. There are always going to be teachers in your school who are emotionally invested in the past and therefore resistant to change. Usually, it's pretty clear which individuals these are and how they will respond to new ideas. Consider informally engaging one of these negative individuals in conversation, either to bring them around to your way of thinking or to figure out how they might fight proposed changes as agents of the culture. Your task is to challenge these individuals' memories of the school's past. Listen to their stories and try to reveal the underlying misconceptions that allow those stories to stay alive. Try to understand where they are coming from by meeting them where they are.

The first week is a good time to start thinking of how to push cultural change during leverage points when the culture is particularly vulnerable. What will you want your staff to communicate? What evidence will you bring to the table describing who we are and who we want to be? Who can tell the best story? What role should the principal play in the early stages of culture shift—the preacher in the pulpit or the man behind the curtain?

Cultures can't lead people into battle; they can only help people feel secure with things as they are. Cultures *manage* people; it takes *people* to *lead* people.

The First Month

Changing a culture requires you to be patient without freezing in place. A few examples of changes in the climate can *feel* like a change in the culture, and it's good to keep these changes in the forefront of people's minds, particularly if they glorify the new vision. The first month is still a time of planting seeds, discussing who you are versus what you want to be, and implementing a purposeful *treatment* that gets you to your goal. It's also a good time to administer the School Culture Survey (see Chapter 6) as a treatment.

Remember: Teachers need to feel as though rewiring the culture is really *their* idea. It's best if the results of the School Culture Survey substantiate conversations that teachers have already begun. Teachers should share any experiences they've had receiving pushback from the culture for trying to implement change and try to understand the reasoning behind this resistance.

Teachers need to feel as though rewiring the culture is really *their* idea.

The First Six Months

In the first six months, be sure to run the School Culture Typology Activity (see Chapter 5). This activity will make more sense to staff once the year is under way and people can better reflect on what is happening in the school. The findings from this activity will help staff clearly see what the existing school culture's strengths and weaknesses are and will give teachers a chance to defend what they are currently doing. Of course, because the activity reveals the culture's weaknesses, the culture itself won't like it.

The First Year

A year is a long time—unless we're talking about geology, astronomy, or culture. You'll be tempted to run the School Culture Survey again at the end of the year to see if anything has changed, but so soon after starting the change process, cultural shifts will be easiest to ascertain by monitoring the behaviors and conversations of teachers. Listen for the stories you planted at the beginning of the year. Are they being shared within and outside of the school? What metaphors and similes are people using to describe this effort? What about to describe *you*?

As you close in on yet another school year, you will have gotten a sense of what strategies for rewiring the culture work best in your particular school. You now know who your allies are and who represents roadblocks to change. Your staff should have the confidence to move forward with new ideas that represent the future while also praising those who have contributed to progress.

CHAPTER 13

Building a School
Culture Rewiring Team

A video by Derek Sivers (2010) titled "First Follower: Leadership Lessons from Dancing Guy" went viral online recently. The video shows how an individual dancing alone in a public place can easily rope others into joining him, building momentum very quickly until a dancing mob forms. The narrator of the video refers to the initial individual as the "lone nut" and provides us with the following theory of crowd-formation that can inform your approach to rewiring your culture:

- The lone nut—that is, the risk-taking, culture-busting leader—stands alone; he or she is Leader #1.
- Leader #1 needs to create a vision that is easy to follow.
- The building of momentum should *not* be about Leader #1, but about everyone onboard with the vision.
- Leader #2 is the first to follow the lone nut—thus transforming the lone nut into a leader.
- Leader #3 is the second to follow Leader #1—the one who motivates the others and helps to create a crowd, giving momentum to the vision. (New followers tend to emulate other followers more than the main leader.)
- When a critical mass of people become followers of the vision, a tipping point is reached—it now becomes risky *not* to join the movement.

We suggest you use this theory to inform the creation of your formal or informal School Culture Rewiring Team.

Creating the Team

School improvement teams are a regular feature in schools these days. They give staff a sense of ownership over what goes on in the building and prevent at least the appearance that the school leader alone is calling the shots from behind closed doors.

In this chapter, we will show you one way to determine which staff members may be best suited to helping you make your vision of a rewired school culture a reality. We are indebted to the following two books for some of the ideas discussed here: *Influencer: The Power to Change Anything* (2007), by Kerry Patterson, Joseph Grenny, David Maxfield, Ron McMillan, and Al Switzler; and *Nexus: Small Worlds and the Groundbreaking Theory of Networks* (2003), by Mike Buchanan.

Step 1: Rating the Teachers

When trying to figure out whom to select for your team, consider rating each teacher in your school according to two main criteria: (1) *effectiveness* and 2) *ability to influence others*. Using the Rating Matrix in Figure 13.1, rate teachers as effective (+3 to +5), average (0 to +2), or ineffective (–1 to –5) along the y-axis of the chart.

When assessing teachers' ability to influence others, you're not looking for used-car salesmen, midway hecklers, or infomercial hosts—you're looking for *people who tell stories that others believe*. After all, cultures are accumulations of stories over time, and the stories are how the culture transmits itself from person to person; they are the currency that the culture uses to articulate its values to the next generation. Using the Rating

Fig 13.1 Teacher Rating Matrix

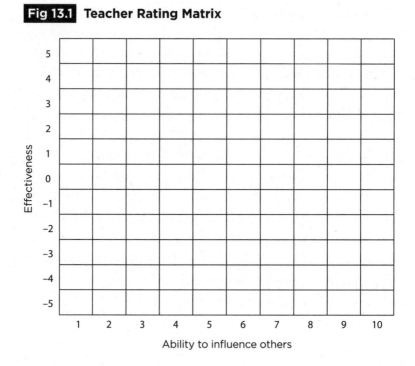

Matrix, rate your teachers' storytelling skills on a scale of 0 to 10 along the x-axis of the chart. The ratings you assign will be highly subjective, and that's fine—use your intuition here. Figure 13.2 shows an example of what the chart might look like once you've rated all the teachers in your school.

Step 2: Connecting the Teachers

Once you've got every teacher plotted as a dot on the chart, the next task is to draw lines between teachers who hang out together, with heavier lines denoting stronger relationships (those who eat together and socialize outside of school) and lighter lines denoting weaker ones (those who may strike up conversations when close to each other but don't seek each

Fig 13.2 Sample Teacher Rating Matrix with Plotted Points

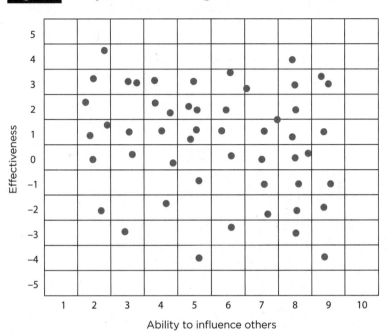

other out for advice). Figure 13.3 shows what the matrix might look like with these relationships made plain.

Once you start plotting any relationships you are aware of among the teachers in your school, you may start to detect patterns. For example, many of the heavier lines may appear to form triangles—perhaps because teachers who share similar degrees of effectiveness cluster together. When you feel you have a fairly representative graph of faculty relationships, identify the individual teachers who are connected to the highest number of colleagues (see Figure 13.4).

Don't let the heavy lines fool you—it's actually the light lines, or weak ties, that will serve us best. As Buchanan (2003) notes,

Fig 13.3 Sample Teacher Rating Matrix Showing Connections among Faculty

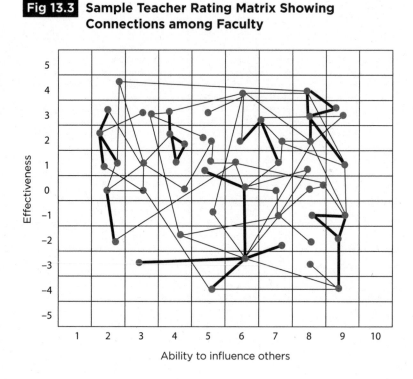

"You can knock out any strong link without having much effect on the 'social distances' within the network" (p. 42). Citing Granovetter, Buchanan refers to any weak link in a network as a social bridge—that is, "a crucial connection that binds a portion of the social fabric together . . . Weak links are often of greater importance than strong links . . . These are the social 'shortcuts' that, if eliminated, would cause the network to fall to pieces" (p. 43).

Step 3: Spreading the Virus

You want your new vision of the culture to spread like a virus among teachers in a school. Among the teachers in your

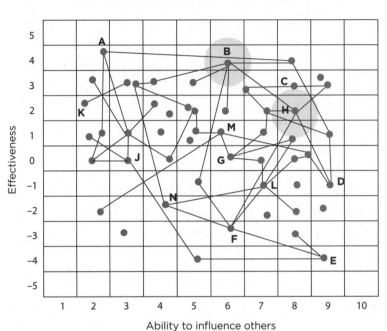

Fig 13.4 **Sample Teacher Rating Matrix Showing Teachers with the Most Connections**

school, which would get the culture spreading the fastest? If you charge only those with the strongest relationships to spread the new vision, chances are it will remain within the group represented by those lines. By contrast, if you charge those with the *weakest* ties to spread the culture, they will do so very quickly.

Present your vision through stories that glorify the future while respecting the past, and send your team out to tell these stories. Your team members have the power not only to tell stories that people believe, but also to listen to any other stories being told among staff. Your team can diagnose the climate of the school.

Don't think of the school improvement team as a group of people who meet once a month to look at data; rather, think of them as *people who interact with all teachers every day.* Team members should seek out and respond to pockets of negativity and make plans to address them. They turn the lone nut into a leader, they clarify the culture's new direction, they build support for the new culture, and they serve as role models for the rest of the school staff.

It's important to understand that *influencers are always influencing*—theirs isn't a hobby, it's a lifestyle. Influencers live for opportunities to share stories with others. Some share stories that align with your plans for moving the culture forward; others tell stories in service of maintaining the status quo. It's up to you to determine which group wins.

Determining the essential few who must be included in either a formal leadership team or informal conversations can make the task ahead more manageable. This team is your offensive line. No quarterback ever got the job done with an average or weak offensive line. You can't change an organizational culture by yourself, and you most likely can't change it without involving these critical influencers.

CHAPTER 14

Leadership Matters

Everyone's heard the stories of the bonuses and golden parachutes that disgraced Wall Street executives receive. How ridiculous to be compensated so obscenely just for putting on a suit and sitting behind a desk all day. No wonder some people think that organizations would be better off without a single leader in charge. And yet those who are the most vocal about how easy being a leader is are often the last to apply for leadership positions, because they know deep down that it isn't easy at all. They know how important a leader can be, especially in stressful situations. And they know how exposed the leader is at all times.

It's much easier to criticize a leader than it is to be one. Negative teachers want to avoid joining the battle for a better school while taking potshots at the risk-takers blazing new trails. Having mistaken their cynicism for wisdom, these negative teachers might very well believe that they're fighting the good fight and protecting the school. They need to be perceived as the weakest members of the new culture.

As we've noted in previous chapters, an organizational culture doesn't require a strong leader to survive. So what effect, if any, can leadership actually have on the culture?

Leadership Is Everything

Everything that happens in an organization reflects the leadership. As the saying goes, "When the leader sneezes, everyone else catches a cold." Think about sports teams, for example: When they struggle, no matter how much we might blame the referee or the crowd, responsibility lies squarely with the coach and with the veterans on the playing field. Same goes in the business world: If a company does poorly, the fault lies with the person at the top. Culture has a tremendous effect on leadership, but leadership makes all the difference.

Factors vs. Fault

State legislation and mandates, funding levels, teachers' unions, students' socioeconomic status, degree of parental involvement: though many different *factors* influence your school culture, the culture is not the *fault* of any one of them. Think about other schools and districts that have faced similar (or even worse) circumstances as yours and managed to overcome them. How did they do it? Leadership.

We recently watched a promotional video from the state department of education that touted the success of a proposed new program by showing footage of a school in which it was very successfully implemented—a school with a very challenging student population. The video showed an enthusiastic faculty and principal hard at work putting the program to work. As we watched the video, we realized that the school's successes were due more to the leadership of its staff than to the vaunted new program. This school had an exemplary principal who was going to make things work for her students regardless of state mandates.

Of course, culture plays a part in a school's successes and failures, too. But it takes the school leader to transform that culture into one that is strong and supportive of student achievement. To do so, leaders must be knowledgeable of the school's traditions and attuned to its cultural nuances.

Filling the Void

When there is a leader but an absence of *leadership*, everybody tries to supply it. Unfortunately, those who tend to do this best are also often the strongest negative personalities in the school. An ineffective principal lends validity to the complaints of naysayers, which enables naysayers to develop much more power than they would under strong leadership. The same applies at the district level: If the superintendent is viewed as ineffective, then the most critical board members will often take a much more assertive role in managing district affairs.

When there is a leader but an absence of *leadership*, everybody tries to supply it.

"Why Don't You Kiss Her Instead Of Talking Her to Death?"

There's a scene in *It's a Wonderful Life* where a young George Bailey hems and haws around his eventual wife, Mary, too nervous to make a move. An older man watching him shouts, "Why don't you kiss her instead of talking her to death?"

Paraphrased—"Why don't you rewire your culture instead of talking about it to death?"—the sentiment applies to schools, too. We can talk about the culture, we can talk about changing the culture, we can talk about the things we need to do before we can change the culture—*or we can just start changing the culture*. Because the culture prefers to stay exactly as it is, announcing your intent to alter it may actually strengthen it. The best offense is one that does not stir up your enemy's defenses.

You can start setting expectations without announcing that they're new. Just set them! This is easiest if it's your first year at a particular school, as staff will expect you to bring some changes. By the same token, once new expectations are set, don't refer to them as new—you want them to seem established.

Keeping Things Positive

Remember that talking up successes makes people feel successful, whereas talking about overwhelming obstacles makes people want to give up. You can further keep things positive in your school by selecting short, upbeat videos or songs to play during staff meetings. Better yet, share stories of compliments that teachers have received. It is critical that you continually remind staff how lucky you all are, how thankful you are, and how fortunate you are to be educators.

Conclusion

Hopefully, reading this book has given you an idea of how to approach rewiring the culture of your school. Though "culture" is a challenging concept to grasp, the effect it has on everything that happens in a school is absolutely tremendous. Developing an awareness of what culture is—being able to understand it, measure it, and change it—is one of the most important things we can do for our students. After all, we don't want our schools just to be different; we want them to be better.

Good luck in the journey. It is one well worth taking.

BIBLIOGRAPHY

Argyris, C. (2010). *Organizational traps: Leadership, culture, organizational design*. New York: Oxford University Press.

Bohannan, P. (1995). *How cultures work*. New York: Free Press.

Buchanan, M. (2003). *Nexus: Small worlds and the groundbreaking theory of networks*. New York: Norton.

Collins, J. (2001). *Good to great: Why some companies make the leap . . . and others don't*. New York: HarperCollins.

Cuban, L. (2003). *Why is it so hard to get good schools?* New York: Teachers College Press.

Deal, T., & Kennedy, A. (1982). *Corporate cultures: The rites and rituals of corporate life*. New York: Addison-Wesley.

Deal, T., & Kennedy, A. (1999). *The new corporate cultures: Revitalizing the workplace after downsizing, mergers, and reengineering*. New York: Basic Books.

Deal, T., & Peterson, K. (2009). *Shaping school culture: Pitfalls, paradoxes, and promises* (2nd ed.). San Francisco: Jossey-Bass.

Dweck, C. (2007). *Mindset: The new psychology of success*. New York: Random House.

Elder, L., & Paul, R. (2012). *30 days to better thinking and better living through critical thinking: A guide for improving every aspect of your life*. Upper Saddle River, NJ: FT Press.

English, F. (2007). *The art of educational leadership: Balancing performance and accountability*. Washington, DC: Sage.

Fullan, M., & Hargreaves, A. (1996). *What's worth fighting for in your school?* New York: Teachers College Press.

Geertz, C. (1973). *The interpretation of cultures*. New York: Basic Books.

Glasser, W. (1999). *Choice theory: A new psychology of personal freedom.* New York: Harper Perennial.

Goffman, E. (1966). *Behavior in public places: Notes on the social organization of gatherings.* New York: Free Press.

Gruenert, S. (2005). Correlations of school culture and student achievement. *NASSP Bulletin, 84*(645), 43–55.

Gruenert, S. & Valentine, J. (2006). School typology activity. Developed at the Middle Level Leadership Center, University of Missouri.

Gruenert, S., & Whitaker, T. (2003). Why do we do what we do? *Instructional Leader, 16*(1), 1–2, 12.

Hachen, D., Jr. (2001). *Sociology in action: Cases for critical thinking and sociological thinking.* Thousand Oaks, CA: Pine Forge Press.

Hargreaves, A. (2000). *Changing teachers, changing times: Teachers' work in the postmodern age.* New York: Teachers College Press.

Heifetz, R., Grashow, A., & Linsky, M. (2009). *The practice of adaptive leadership.* Boston: Harvard Business Publishing.

Hofstede, G. (1997). *Culture and organizations: Software for the mind.* New York: McGraw-Hill.

Hofstede, G., Hofstede, J. G., & Minkov, M. (2010). *Cultures and organizations: Software of the mind* (3rd ed.). New York: McGraw-Hill.

Horowitz, H. (1987). *Campus life: Undergraduate cultures from the end of the eighteenth century to the present.* Chicago: University of Chicago Press.

Islam, G., & Zyphur, M. J. (2009). Rituals in organizations: A review and expansion of current theory. *Group & Organization Management, 34,* 114.

Keyton, J. (2005). *Communication and organizational culture: A key to understanding work experiences.* Thousand Oaks, CA: Roxbury Publishing.

Kuh, G. & Whitt, E. (1988). The invisible tapestry: Culture in American universities and colleges. *ASHE-ERIC Higher Education Reports, 17*(1).

Lewin, K. (1951). *Field theory in social science: Selected theoretical papers.* New York: Harper & Row.

Lortie, D. (1975). *Schoolteacher.* Chicago: University of Chicago.

Martin, J. (2001). *Organizational culture: Mapping the terrain.* Washington, DC: Sage.

Maslow, A. (1943). A theory of human motivation. *Psychological Review, 50*(4), 370–396.

Milgram, S. (1963). Behavioral study of obedience. *Journal of Abnormal and Social Psychology, 67*(4), 371–378.

Morgan, G. (1986). *Images of organizations.* Beverly Hills, CA: Sage.

Ouchi, W., & Wilkins, A. (1985). Organizational culture. *Annual Review of Sociology, 11,* 457–483.

Patterson, K., Grenny, J., Maxfield, D., McMillan, R., & Switzler, A. (2008). *Influencer: The power to change anything.* New York: McGraw-Hill.

Peters, T., & Waterman, R. (2006). *In search of excellence.* New York: Harper Business.

Peterson, K. (1994). *Building collaborative cultures: Seeking ways to reshape urban schools.* Naperville, IL: NCREL.

Peterson, M. W., Cameron, K. S., Mets, L. A., Jones, P., & Ettington, D. (1986). *The organizational context for teaching and learning: A review of research literature.* Ann Arbor, MI: National Center for Research to Improve Postsecondary Teaching and Learning.

Pounder, D. (1998). *Restructuring schools for collaboration: Promises and pitfalls.* Albany: State University of New York Press.

Ray, W. (2001). *The logic of culture: Authority and identity in the modern era.* Hoboken, NJ: Wiley.

Rohn, J. (n.d.). Quote taken from http://www.goodreads.com/quotes/1798-you-are-the-average-of-the-five-people-you-spend.

Rosenberg, T. (2011). *Join the club: How peer pressure can transform the world.* New York: Norton.

Sarason, S. (1996). *Revisiting the school and the problem of change.* New York: Teachers College Press.

Sathe, V. (1983). Implications of corporate culture: A manager's guide to action. *Organizational Dynamics, 12*(2), 5–23.

Schein, E. (1992). *Organizational culture and leadership* (2nd ed.). San Francisco: Jossey-Bass.

Senge, P., Cambron-McCabe, N., Lucas, T., & Smith, B. (2012). *Schools that learn: A fifth discipline fieldbook for educators, parents, and everyone who cares about education.* New York: Crown Business.

Sergiovanni, T. (1990). *Value-added leadership: How to get extraordinary performance in schools.* New York: Harcourt Brace Jovanovich.

Sivers, D. (2010). First follower: Leadership lessons from dancing guy [video]. Available: https://www.youtube.com/watch?v=fW8amMCVAJQ.

Turner, E. (2013). *What effective principals do to improve instruction and increase student achievement* [doctoral dissertation]. Indiana State University, Terre Haute, Indiana.

Van Maanen, J., & Barley, S. (1985). Occupational communities: Culture and control in organizations. *Research in Organizational Behavior, 6,* 287–365.

Wagner, T. (1994). *How schools change.* Boston: Beacon Press.

Whitaker, T. (2011). *What great principals do differently* (2nd ed.). Larchmont, NY: Eye on Education.

Whitaker, T., Whitaker, B., & Lumpa, D. (2008). *Motivating and inspiring teachers: The education leader's guide for building staff morale* (2nd ed.). Larchmont, NY: Eye on Education.

INDEX

Note: Page locators followed by an italicized *f* indicate information contained in figures.

ABOUT THE AUTHORS

 **Steve Gruenert** is the department chair of the Educational Leadership department at Indiana State University (ISU). He helped design the Indiana Principal Leadership Institute, has coordinated the Principal Preparation Program at ISU, and has been a principal at both the high school and middle school levels. His research passion is school culture and climate, and he continues to engage with leaders at the national and international levels, helping them to think about the role of culture in school improvement.

 **Todd Whitaker** has been fortunate to blend his passion with his profession. He is a leading presenter in the field of education and a professor of educational leadership at Indiana State University. He has previously served as both a teacher and a principal and is the author of over 30 books, including *What Great Teachers Do Differently, The 10-Minute In-Service,* and *Shifting the Monkey.* Todd and his wife, Beth, have three children: Katherine, Madeline, and Harrison.

Related ASCD Resources: School Culture

At the time of publication, the following ASCD resources were available (ASCD stock numbers appear in parentheses). For up-to-date information about ASCD resources, go to www.ascd .org.

Networks

Visit the ASCD Web site (www.ascd.org) and search for "networks" for information about professional educators who have formed groups around topics like "School Culture." Look in the "Network Directory" for current facilitators' addresses and phone numbers.

ASCD EDge Group

Exchange ideas and connect with other educators interested in school culture on the social networking site ASCD EDge™ at http://ascdedge.ascd.org/

Print Products

Building Shared Responsibility for Student Learning Anne Conze-mius and Jan O'Neill (#101039)

Finding Your Leadership Style: A Guide for Educators Jeffrey Glanz (#102115)

The Learning Leader: How to Focus School Improvement for Better Results Douglas B. Reeves (#105151)

Reframing Teacher Leadership to Improve Your School Douglas B. Reeves (#108012)

School Climate Change: How Do I Build a Positive Environment for Learning? Peter DeWitt and Sean Slade (#SF114084)

The Whole Child Initiative helps schools and communities create learning environments that allow students to be healthy, safe, engaged, supported, and challenged. To learn more about other books and resources that relate to the whole child, visit www.wholechildeducation.org.

For more information: send e-mail to member@ascd.org; call 1-800-933-2723 or 703-578-9600, press 2; send a fax to 703-575-5400; or write to Information Services, ASCD, 1703 N. Beauregard St., Alexandria, VA 22311-1714 USA.